The Science of Fashion

JULIE DANNEBERG

Illustrated by Michelle Simpson

Nomad Press

A division of Nomad Communications

10 9 8 7 6 5 4 3 2 1

This book was manufactured by CGB Printers,
North Mankato, Minnesota, United States
August 2021, Job #1024084

ISBN Softcover: 978-1-64741-030-8
ISBN Hardcover: 978-1-64741-027-8

Educational Consultant, Marla Conn

Questions regarding the ordering of this book should be addressed to
Nomad Press
PO Box 1036, Norwich, VT 05055
www.nomadpress.net

Printed in the United States.

More science titles from the Inquire & Investigate series

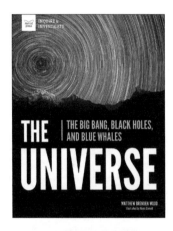

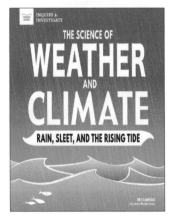

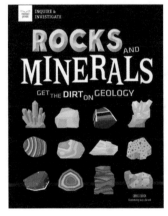

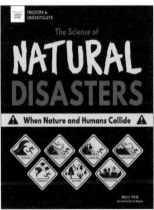

Contents ▶

Glossary ▼ Metric Conversions
Resources ▼ Selected Bibliography ▼ Index

1733: John Kay invents the flying shuttle, which allows a single worker to weave much wider fabrics. Carrying the weft threads, the bullet-shaped shuttle flies back and forth over the warp threads on the loom.

1742: The first cotton mill opens in England.

1764: James Hargreaves invents the spinning jenny. This improves on the spinning wheel, as it lets a single worker spin eight spools at once.

1769: Richard Arkwright patents the water frame, a spinning wheel powered by a water wheel. The water wheel provides power to the spinning frame, allowing for an unbelievable 128 spools of yarn to be spun at the same time.

1785: Edmund Cartwright patents the mechanized power loom.

1790: The first steam-powered textile factory is built in Nottingham, England.

1792: Eli Whitney invents the cotton gin, an automated machine that quickly and easily separates cotton fibers from cotton seeds.

1793: Samuel Slater and his partner, Moses Brown, build the first successful cotton spinning mill in Pawtucket, Rhode Island.

1804: Joseph Marie Jacquard, a French weaver, invents the Jacquard Loom, which can weave complex designs automatically using a punch card technology that controls the weaving of the cloth.

1830: Barthélemy Thimonnier, a French tailor, invents the first functional sewing machine.

1850: Twelve-year-old Margaret Knight, eventually known as the "female Edison" because of her many inventions, invents a safety device for the loom after witnessing a man being injured at a textile factory.

1856: William Henry Perkin invents the first synthetic dye.

1883: Jan Matzeliger, a Black man originally from Paramaribo, Suriname, receives a patent for a shoe-lasting machine that increases the shoe-making capability of a factory from 50 to 700 shoes per day.

1953: Dupont produces the first commercial polyester fiber.

1965: Stephanie Kwolek invents the synthetic material that will later be developed into Kevlar.

1972: The Hamilton Watch Co. and Electro/Data Inc. develop the first digital watch.

1989: Reebok Pump is the first shoe equipped with an internal inflation system.

2011: Levi's introduces Water<Less Jeans, a collection that creates a water savings during manufacturing of 28 percent to 96 percent, depending on the style.

2013: Massachusetts Institute of Technology (MIT) releases a study that details the negative impact of the shoe industry on the environment.

2020: Thanks to the COVID-19 pandemic, masks become a fashion accessory.

2021: The Black fashion designer Sergio Hudson creates outfits for former First Lady Michelle Obama and Vice President Kamala Harris to wear at the inauguration of U.S. President Joe Biden.

Introduction ▶
Fashion Through History

FASHION IS CULTURE, LANGUAGE, EXPRESSION, HISTORY, AND SO MUCH MORE!

What part do science and engineering play in the fashion industry?

From sewing machines to synthetic dyes, science and engineering have made the fashion industry possible. Through time, people have been inspired to invent new methods of producing fabric and putting it together in ways that reflect the values and needs of their culture.

What are you wearing right now? Jeans, joggers, sneakers, a vintage shirt, and sunglasses? What about earrings? Your fashion choices play an important part in your life. They help shape the world's impression of you, support your sense of belonging in various groups such as a sports team or cultural club, and define your comfort levels, both physically and emotionally.

Have you ever worn an outfit that felt okay when you put it on in the morning, but by midday, you wanted to get it off? Do you have a certain outfit that you wear whenever you need a confidence boost? That's the power of fashion.

The daily ritual of picking out the day's outfit is probably part of your morning routine. But how often do you actually think about how fashion affects your everyday life or how your choices go beyond your personal world? Do you ever wonder how the creation of the clothes in your closet influences global economies or impacts the earth's environment?

You might be thinking, "Seriously? Global economies and the environment? It's just a T-shirt and a pair of jeans. What's the big deal?"

Who knew fashion was so important?

FASHION CHOICES: IT'S GLOBAL

The newest fashions in 1829

The truth is, fashion is a big deal, especially when combined with the choices of everyone else in your school, your city, and your country. Whether you are a fashionista or a wear-the-same-thing-every-day kind of person, your clothing choices are just a small piece in a worldwide puzzle.

Clothing choices affect global economics because fashion is a $1.2-trillion industry, employing millions of people all over the world. Your choices affect the environment because the fashion industry is one of the largest polluters in the world, second only to the oil industry.

Finally, your fashion choices affect and are affected by the world of science and engineering. Everything you wear is the product of a long line of scientific and technological advances. These include the highly automated machines fabric is made on, the synthetic fabrics created in a lab, and the engineering behind smart textiles.

Fashion today

Science, engineering, technology, and fashion are truly interwoven in a mutually beneficial and reciprocal way. In other words, the continued growth of the fashion industry is dependent on the knowledge and technology gained from scientists and engineers. On the flip side, the scientific, engineering, and technological advances gained in the fashion industry are applied to other fields and industries.

The combined efforts of science, engineering, and fashion have created a global industry that affects people, economies, and environments all around the world.

CHA-CHING

The fashion industry is an economic powerhouse in today's global economy. As of 2015, according to the Joint Economic Committee of the U.S. Congress, fashion is a $1.2-trillion industry. More than $250 billion is spent on fashion annually in the United States alone. Start to finish, from making textiles to selling clothing in stores, the fashion industry employs more than 60 million people globally.

CLOTHING CHOICE: IT'S PERSONAL

True, fashion is a global industry, but fashion is also personal. Obviously, you wear clothing to protect yourself from the elements. However, there are other, less obvious factors that influence your clothing and fashion choices.

One important factor is whether your choice is socially acceptable for the community or culture in which you live.

In all cultures, there is a sense of what is viewed as appropriate and inappropriate clothing for work and school, for adults and kids. If your clothes don't fit into that, you might be stared at, judged, or even punished for being "different."

Often, schools and work environments have dress codes that outline the appropriate clothing choices for that environment.

This idea of socially acceptable clothing applies to peer groups as well. Think about your group of friends. Chances are, no one has handed out a printed dress code of what you can and cannot wear, but if you take a look around, you will see that everyone sticks pretty close to the unspoken dress code, whether that's jeans and T-shirts, high-end athletic leisurewear, or cowboy boots and a cowboy hat.

Religious affiliation might also decide, or at least influence, what you can and cannot wear. For instance, a hijab is worn in public by some Muslim women. A conservative Christian community might not allow girls to wear short shorts or short skirts, while men in Amish communities might be required to wear specially made dark suits without lapels that fasten with hooks rather than buttons.

A person's choice of clothing is also dependent on the day's activities. High heels and tight pants might be a perfect outfit to wear for a job as a salesperson in a high-end clothing store, but might not be the smartest choice for a construction site or for lawn work. If your day involves a special occasion, there might be some fashion requirements for that, too.

SCIENTIFIC METHOD

The scientific method is the process scientists use to ask questions and find answers. Keep a science journal to record your methods and observations during all the activities in this book. You can use a scientific method worksheet to keep your ideas and observations organized.

Question: What are we trying to find out? What problem are we trying to solve?

Research: What is already known about this topic?

Hypothesis: What do we think the answer will be?

Equipment: What supplies are we using?

Method: What procedure are we following?

Results: What happened and why?

PRIMARY SOURCES

Primary sources come from people who were eyewitnesses to events. They might write about the event, take pictures, post short messages to social media or blogs, or record the event for radio or video. The photographs in this book are primary sources, taken at the time of the event. Paintings of events are usually not primary sources, since they were often painted long after the event took place. What other primary sources can you find? Why are primary sources important? Do you learn differently from primary sources than from secondary sources, which come from people who did not directly experience the event?

Some clothes, such as sports or school uniforms, show your identity as a member or supporter of a team. Others show your profession, such as a doctor's white lab coat or a firewomen's uniform or a judge's black robes.

Interestingly, all of these choices have to do with social belonging, or working to be acceptable to or part of a group. Psychologists say this is a fundamental human need and is related to a sense of happiness and well-being. Fashion and clothing choices are one way that we signal and reinforce that feeling of belonging.

As you can see, fashion choices are about a lot more than just covering our bodies. Clothing tells the world who you are, what you like, and, often, what socioeconomic group you are in.

A printed metal fabric designed by NASA engineers to be used in space

Credit: NASA/JPL-Caltech

The story you are telling about yourself through your clothing might be a true representation of who you are or it might be a made-up version of the person you want the world to see. Your clothing choices might make you look richer than you are, more athletic, older, younger, wild, or conservative. It is your story to tell.

A LITTLE FASHION HISTORY

The history of fashion and clothing can be divided into two periods—before the Industrial Revolution and after the Industrial Revolution. In both periods, science, engineering, and technology played a role. However, during and after the Industrial Revolution, thanks to innovations in technology, changes began happening faster and faster. These changes even helped eventually create the idea of fashion in the first place.

It is important to note that the history of clothing is not the same thing as the history of fashion.

When we say the word "clothing," we are simply referring to the items that are worn on the body. Fashion, however, has a somewhat different meaning. The word "fashion" refers to certain styles of dressing. These styles vary with different periods of time and different cultures, depending on the values of people at that time and place.

Think about it—a pair of pants is merely a piece of clothing that is worn to cover the lower part of the body. However, when you think about pants in terms of fashion, the pants wealthy gentlemen wore in England in 1750 are quite different from the pants worn by Western ranchers in 1900.

One way scientists get involved in fashion is to study the effect of fashion choices on the individual. Take a look at what one study revealed.

Do you think you make judgments based on clothing?

PT clothes saying

Claire Distenfeld, owner of Fivestory, which is one of New York City's hippest fashion boutiques, says that fashion is "a form of expression without the use of words."

A CLOSE-UP ON CLOSETS

For most of human history, closets were not built into houses. There was no need, since most people stored their one or two extra sets of clothing in dressers. If you were rich and had lots of room and lots of clothing, you might have a free-standing closet called a wardrobe. In fact, America's first built-in closets didn't show up until the late 1800s. The first advertised built-in closets were found in the Dakota Apartment Building in New York City, New York. Advertised as 2½ feet deep and 6 feet wide, these closets were the height of luxury.

Both of those are vastly different from the joggers and blue jeans we wear today, all in the name of fashion.

Anthropologists believe that humans began wearing clothes as protection from the elements between 100,000 and 500,000 years ago. Those earliest clothes were made from animal skin, fur, or leaves that were probably wrapped, draped, or tied around their bodies.

Technology entered the picture at least 50,000 years ago. That's when simple sewing needles made from animal bones were used to sew several skins or furs together to make a more fitted garment.

Researchers have found evidence of primitive looms dating to around 5000 BCE. These looms mean that ancient humans had figured out a way to turn raw materials into cloth.

As centuries passed, bit by bit, culture by culture, societies slowly began to come up with more sophisticated ways to make textiles and clothing. Still, every piece of clothing was made by hand. First, the cotton or flax or sheep had to be raised, and then their fiber was harvested, cleaned, and spun into yarn or thread. That yarn was woven into a piece of material that was then cut and sewn by hand into a simple piece of clothing.

We will learn more about this process in the next chapter, but making clothing was certainly an extremely labor-intensive endeavor. Layer that in with all of the other work a person needed to do to survive, since there were no quick runs to the grocery store, no electric furnaces, and no construction companies to build homes. People had to raise food, chop wood for heat, and build their own shelters.

You can see that having a closet full of clothes to choose from each morning in order to get ready to go to school—though school wasn't a daily reality for most people—was not a feasible option. Even the richest people, who could afford to have others make their clothing for them, didn't have the luxury of having lots of different outfits in their closet. In fact, they didn't have closets either.

THE INDUSTRIAL REVOLUTION CHANGES EVERYTHING

When the Industrial Revolution occurred, everything changed in a fairly short amount of time. These changes began in Great Britain in the late 1700s, but eventually spread around the world in the mid-to-late 1800s.

ENGINEERING DESIGN PROCESS

Engineers recognize, define, and analyze problems. They use science and math to solve these problems, often creating special technology or tools in the process. This method of problem solving is called the engineering design process. This approach recognizes that there might be several solutions to a problem. Engineers choose an option, test it, evaluate it, and adjust. Many engineers use a worksheet like this one to keep their thoughts organized.

Problem: What problem are we trying to solve?

Research: Has anything been invented to help solve the problem? What can we learn?

Brainstorm: Draw lots of designs for your device and list the materials you are using!

Prototype: Build the design you drew during brainstorming.

Test: Test your prototype and record your observations.

Evaluate: Analyze your test results. Do you need to make adjustments? Do you need to try a different prototype?

TRAITOR OR KEEN BUSINESSMAN?

Samuel Slater (1768–1835) was dubbed the "Father of the American Industrial Revolution" by U.S. President Andrew Jackson (1767–1845). In Great Britain, however, he was called "Slater the Traitor." As a teen growing up in Milford, England, Slater worked as an apprentice in a textile factory, where he memorized the designs of the machinery. In 1790, a 21-year-old Slater emigrated to the United States and convinced the owner of a textile mill that he was an expert at building textile machinery. Turns out, he was! Slater soon built, from memory, several of the machines he had worked on as an apprentice. By 1793, having gone into business with that same owner, he established the first successful textile mill in the United States.

Thanks to scientific and technological advances, societies changed from rural and agrarian communities where everything was made by hand. They became industrial societies where engines and machines could more efficiently and effectively do the work once done by individuals. As time went on, advances in engineering and technology introduced new methods and machines.

Several innovations stand out as truly important in catapulting clothing manufacturing into the future.

Prior to the spinning jenny (invented in 1765), the spinning of fiber into yarn was generally done at home. One person sat at a spinning wheel, painstakingly spinning a single spool of yarn. It was slow and tedious work!

The spinning jenny was a hand-powered spinning machine that allowed a single spinner to operate eight spools at once, thus reducing the amount of work required to make yarn. This invention was soon replaced by the water frame, which was powered by a water wheel. Patented by Richard Arkwright (1732–1792) in 1769, the water frame could spin 128 spools at a time. Since yarn is woven together or knitted to make cloth, the more yarn that is spun, the more cloth that can be made.

The next innovation was the power loom, designed in 1784 by Edmund Cartwright (1743–1823) and built in 1785. Power looms made the production of cloth faster and required much less human labor. The more cloth that was made, the more demand there was for it.

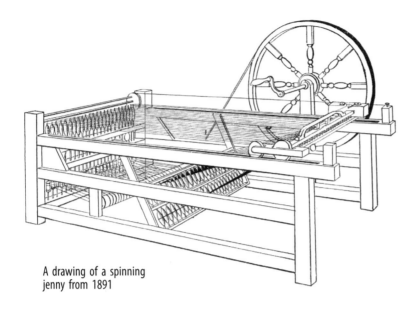

A drawing of a spinning jenny from 1891

Take a look of some of the marvelous machines invented during the Industrial Revolution.

Can you spot the spinning jenny?

ThoughtCo Industrial Revolution

Great Britain, home of these inventions, soon had a flourishing textile industry that controlled the world textile market. In order to protect their inventions and their businesses, Great Britain created laws that made it illegal to send their machines overseas or for textile mill workers to move to other countries.

The cotton gin, invented by Eli Whitney (1765–1825), was another significant technological step. Patented in 1794, it created an automatic way to remove the cotton fiber from the cotton seeds. This provided a much quicker means to harvest cotton, which in turn allowed the American South to plant more cotton.

The invention of the cotton gin also created the need for more slaves to tend the crops. Had the cotton gin not been invented, slavery might have ended sooner in American history.

A cotton gin at work in the 1940s

Many of the people mentioned in history are white men. Why? They had better access to education and opportunity. People of color and women were denied opportunity through formal laws and regulations as well as societal prejudice. Before the Civil War, it was illegal for slaves in the South to get an education, own land, and obtain patents on the inventions they created. After the Civil War, Black people still faced discrimination and prejudice. But that doesn't mean Black people weren't inventing. You can read some of those stories at this website.

How are people of color still affected by prejudice today?

Nat Geo African
American inventors

The sewing machine has a long and complicated history of invention. Many inventors took a swing at it, including Elias Howe (1819–1892), who patented his lockstitch machine in 1846. Initially, it did not sell well, but with modifications and improvements from Isaac Singer (1811–1875) and Allen Wilson (1824–1888), the final version worked more easily and efficiently. The first home sewing machine was sold in 1889.

Before the invention of the sewing machine, seamstresses sewed each piece of clothing by hand, individually fitting it to each customer. An experienced seamstress could sew about 40 to 50 stitches per minute, while the new sewing machines could sew about 900 stitches per minute. The time per outfit went down greatly, which meant profit went up.

What about making the fabric beautiful? Long before dyes were made in laboratories, they were made in homes from natural resources such as fruits and berries and nuts. The first synthetic, or manmade, dye was accidentally created in 1856 by an 18-year-old British chemist named William Henry Perkin (1838–1907).

Perkin was attempting to create a synthetic version of quinine, a plant used to treat malaria. Instead, he came up with a mixture that made a purple dye that would eventually become very popular in Great Britain. This discovery led to more work by other chemists trying to create different synthetic dyes.

FABRIC FACT

Synthetic fabrics now fill everyone's closets, but rayon, the first manmade fabric, wasn't available commercially until 1910. Nylon came along in 1939 and disco dancers and bike racers were thrilled to welcome spandex into the world in the 1970s.

Child labor was commonly used in cotton mills. Children's small hands and fingers could be useful working in machines where adult-sized hands wouldn't fit.

Credit: Lewis Hine

Often, when people think of the jobs in the fashion industry, they immediately think of a fashion designer. And, of course, the fashion industry is dependent on the skills and vision of these creative people. But it is important to remember that fashion designers do not work alone. Beside them work a whole fleet of science, technology, engineering, and math (STEM) professionals.

The fashion industry has many branches and requires many types of skill sets. In this book, we'll explore the role science, engineering, and technology play in the fashion industry, including changes in fabric, color, design, accessories, and shoes. We'll also look at some of the different jobs and specialties that keep fashion growing and changing.

Ready to stroll down the runway? Let's go!

KEY QUESTIONS

- **How did the Industrial Revolution change the clothing and fashion industry?**

- **Why do we know less about women and Black people in the history of textiles?**

- **What is the relationship between fashion designers and textile manufacturers?**

TEXT TO WORLD

How is the clothing that you wear to school different from the clothing you wear to play sports? Why?

THE STEM IN YOUR CLOSET

Have you ever really thought about what kinds of science, engineering, and technology actually go into making your clothes? Now is your chance! The zipper on your jacket was at one time an engineering miracle. The shirt that has built-in protection from the sun's ultraviolet rays is a scientific innovation that helps to keep you healthy. There is a world of science and engineering in your closet. Just open the door.

- **Look at your closet through an inquisitive science and engineering lens.** Keep in mind the topics covered in this book: fabric, color, design, accessories, and shoes.

- **Make a list of the technological or scientific advancements that you notice.** You don't have to explain them all, just notice what are there and record them in your science journal.

- **Choose one advancement you found in your closet and research its history.** Who invented it? Why? How did that invention change the industry? Has anyone invented something that replaces that innovation?

VOCAB LAB

Write down what you think each word means. What root words can you find to help you? What does the context of the word tell you?

economy, **engineering**, **fashion**, **patent**, **prototype**, **synthetic**, and **textile**.

Compare your definitions with those of your friends or classmates. Did you all come up with the same meanings? Turn to the text and glossary if you need help.

To investigate more, choose one of the inventors or innovators that designed something in your closet. Were they male or female? Were they recognized for their contributions? Were they paid for their invention? Why does it matter?

Chapter 1 ▶

Textiles and Technology

What are textiles and how are they made?

Creating the fabric that clothes are made of is a long and complex process, no matter if the fabric is natural or synthetic.

Your morning begins when the alarm goes off. You throw off the sheets, pull back the curtains, and shuffle across the soft carpet to the bathroom, where you wash your face and brush your hair. You rewrap the ace bandage around the ankle you twisted yesterday during volleyball practice when you came down from spiking the ball over the net.

It's snowing outside, but luckily, your insulated room is nice and warm. After getting dressed and eating breakfast, you grab your backpack, get into the car, buckle your seatbelt, and head off to school.

Textiles are a part of your everyday life.

Can you list the textiles named in the above paragraph? You probably already know that clothing, curtains, and sheets are made from textiles. What about the carpet, the bristles in your hairbrush, the ace bandage, the fiberglass insulation, your backpack, the volleyball net, and the seatbelt?

Textiles include a wide range of products that you encounter throughout your day, such as toothbrush bristles and seatbelts. Since this book is about clothing and fashion, we're going to focus on textiles that you can wear and use the terms "textile" and "fabric" interchangeably.

TEXTILES: THE BASICS

Tiny, thin, threadlike structures called fibers are the raw material of textiles. Fibers can be natural and manufactured, or manmade. Natural fibers come from plants and animals and even worms! Cotton, flax, and hemp are plant fibers used to make cloth. Wool comes from sheep, goats, and alpaca, and silkworms are the source of silk.

Manufactured fibers come from substances that were not originally a fiber. Manufactured fibers can be regenerated or synthetic. Regenerated cellulose fiber is made from plant or wood pulp and needs additional chemical treatments to become a usable fiber. Synthetic fibers such as polyester and nylon are made from a petroleum-based chemical mixture. In addition, some textiles are a mix of natural and synthetic fibers, such as polyester-cotton blends.

The basic steps for making textiles have not evolved much since they were first developed, even though production methods have changed thanks to technology. First, the fibers are harvested, gathered, or made, depending on what type of fibers they are.

Cotton fibers are harvested, wool and silk are gathered, and regenerated cellulose or synthetic fibers are made.

A silkworm cocoon

A thirteenth-century painting of women placing silkworms on trays together with mulberry leaves

Credit: Liang Kai

The natural fibers are cleaned and carded. Both natural and synthetic fibers are then spun into thread or yarn and woven into cloth.

Textile manufacturing, however, is just a single piece of the global fashion industry. The cotton for your T-shirt might have been grown in the American South, made into cloth in China, dyed in Bangladesh, cut and sewn into a T-shirt in India, and then shipped back to the United States, where it appears in stores across the country. This string of processes is called a supply chain. It's the system of people, resources, businesses, and manufacturing required to transform raw material into a finished product and get it into the hands of a consumer. The creation of a piece of clothing has a long, multi-step supply chain.

In the textile industry, "yarn" is the result of twisting or spinning fibers together into a continuous strand. The width of the final strand varies, depending on the type of textile being made.

NATURAL FIBERS

Cotton is the most widely used plant fiber—an estimated 50 percent of the clothing worn in the world is made from cotton. In the United States, this plant is grown in the warm, Southern states. When the cotton plant becomes mature, the cotton bolls open, revealing clumps of soft, white fibers attached to the cotton seeds.

Once harvested, cotton undergoes ginning, which separates the cotton fibers from the seeds and cleans it of dirt and debris. After the cotton fiber is cleaned, it is carded, or brushed, to make the loose fibers all face the same way. This process leaves the cotton looking like a large, fluffy mat. It is then rolled up and sent to a textile mill, where it is made into cloth.

Wool comes mostly from sheep, but also from goats, llamas, and alpacas, which are raised specifically for their fleece. The shearing of sheep takes place in the spring, when the fleece is cut off the sheep in a single piece. It takes only four minutes for an expert shearer to shear one sheep! After removal, the fleece is thoroughly washed to remove both dirt and lanolin, a natural grease that keeps the sheep's coat dry. Once it is washed, the fibers are separated out and then carded in preparation for spinning.

Lanolin is used in skin lotions and body creams as a moisturizer.

Watch this video about how cotton is harvested for textile manufacturing. Keep in mind that each step initially presented a problem that an engineer had to solve.

What are some of the solutions people came up with?

Science Channel cotton

FABRIC FACT
◇◇◇◇◇◇◇◇◇

Wool can be found in some unusual places. The covering on a tennis ball and the tip of a felt-tipped pen are both made of felted wool.

SOFT, SOFTER, SOFTEST

To make softer, finer yarns, the short fibers of the cotton are separated or combed out before spinning. Those short fibers are then used to make products such as cotton balls and Q-tips. Yarns are identified by number. The higher the number, the finer (thinner) the yarn and the softer the finished fabric feels. Therefore, 800 thread-count sheets are softer than 500 thread-count sheets.

Silkworms are raised just for their fiber. The adult silkworm moth lays its eggs on mulberry leaves. When the caterpillars hatch out of the eggs, they eat the leaves. During several weeks, the caterpillars eat and grow and eat and grow, until they are ready to spin their cocoons.

Silkworms make and then spit out a delicate silk thread from two tiny holes called spinnerets, which are located below their mouths. Once inside the cocoon, the silkworm slowly turns into a moth. To harvest the silk, the cocoons are taken and boiled, killing the silkworm inside and loosening the "glue" that holds the cocoon together. These silk fibers are gently unwound from the cocoon, ready for spinning.

Each silkworm's cocoon consists of one long fiber, called a filament, that is more than 1,000 feet long, with some stretching up to 3,000 feet.

To make 1 pound of silk, 1,500 silkworms must consume 100 pounds of mulberry leaves.

It takes someone 40 hours of spinning by hand to make one pound of silk thread. About 110 cocoons make enough silk for a necktie and 620 for a blouse. Almost 5,000 cocoons are needed to make enough silk for one long dress.

Once the natural fibers are gathered and prepared, they are ready to be turned into yarn through a process called spinning. Cotton and wool fibers are short and thin, and the silk filaments are long, but they all need to be stretched and twisted together to make one longer, stronger, thicker strand of yarn. As it is spun, the yarn is wrapped onto huge spools.

The Costume of Yorkshire, 1814
Credit: George Walker

Before the Industrial Revolution, the spinning of natural fiber into yarn was done by hand on a spinning wheel—an extremely labor-intensive activity! Some of the earliest technological innovations of the Industrial Revolution had to do with creating machines that made the process of spinning yarn more efficient.

MANUFACTURED FIBER

Regenerated cellulose fiber is made from cellulose pulp that has been extracted from plants or wood. After being treated chemically, it ends up as a syrupy liquid. In a process called wet spinning, the syrupy liquid is pushed through a spinneret and then through a bath of sulfuric acid, which solidifies the liquid into long, thin, usable fibers.

Watch this video on the process of making cotton.

Can you keep track of how many different steps and machines are required to make yarn that is ready for weaving?

how made cotton yarn

Do you have a shirt made of rayon? Rayon is made from regenerated cellulose.

Synthetic fibers, including nylon, polyester, and spandex, are made from a petroleum-based chemical mixture. Although the chemical recipe changes depending on the type of synthetic textile being made, the process is similar for all of them.

To make synthetic fibers, the chemicals are first heated to form a liquid made up of very long molecules called polymers. As with the regenerated cellulose mixture, the liquid is forced through a spinneret, which changes the liquid chemical concoction into long filaments. As the filaments cool, they harden and are stretched through a series of rollers, then wound onto a spool to get them ready for weaving.

IT'S ALL CHEMISTRY

Cellulose is a natural polymer made up of glucose units. It is the main component of the cell walls of most plants and is insoluble in water. A polymer is a substance with a molecular structure made up of a string of similar units bonded together. Synthetic textiles are made from manmade polymers in a process called polymerization.

PUTTING IT ALL TOGETHER

Once the yarn is ready, the preparatory work for creating textiles is done. The next step is to use that yarn to make the fabric. Weaving and knitting are the two main ways to manufacture textiles.

People have been weaving for thousands of years.

With the introduction of the power loom, weaving textiles became much faster and easier, which meant fabric grew more available for less money. Here's how weaving works.

The lengthwise, or warp, threads are held taut on a beam, while the widthwise, or weft, threads are carried by a shuttle that moves across the fabric. The shuttle weaves the weft threads under and over alternating warp threads. Sometimes, the yarn is dyed before weaving, and the pattern is woven in as the textile is manufactured. Textiles are also often dyed or printed with patterns after being woven.

While early looms used a shuttle to carry the weft threads, in 1927, the more efficient shuttle-less loom came into use. Today, we have a variety of looms, including air-jet looms that use a jet of air to propel the weft thread across the warp, and rapier looms that weave with finger-like carriers called rapiers. It is important to note that although weaving technology has advanced, the basics of weaving are still the same.

Another way of creating textiles with yarn is by knitting. This can be done by hand with knitting needles or by a high-speed knitting machine. Knitted fabric is more stretchy and loose than woven fabric because of its loops. Whether done by hand or by machine, knitting uses one continuous length of yarn with one stitch connected to the next stitch and one row connected to the next row through connecting loops.

Weft knitting is the type of knitting done to make a lot of clothing. The cloth is knitted and then, just as with woven material, the pieces are cut out and sewn together. You may think of knitting as applying only to sweaters or scarves, but many types of clothing can be knitted—even T-shirts—with very delicate yarn.

THE SILK ROAD

The process of making silk was invented in China, and for a long time, that knowledge was not shared with the outside world. Starting in the second century BCE, silk was traded on routes that connected the East and the West. These routes were known as the Silk Road. As traders traveled through different countries and traded unique goods from their own countries, they also exchanged knowledge of culture, religion, and politics. This is a practice called globalization that still goes on today through international business.

Check out this video to learn more. Why did culture, religion, and ideas travel alongside material goods?

Seeker Silk Road

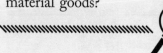

Many people find knitting and weaving to be a relaxing hobby that produces beautiful clothing!

PS

According to Zoe Hong, a fashion industry specialist, "fabrics and fiber technology are the true future of fashion." Watch this longer video for an in-depth explanation of the textile manufacturing supply chain and to gain a deeper understanding of the qualities of different types of fabric.

What might she mean when she says there is no limit to fiber technology?

Hong Fabrics 1

Once a fabric is woven or knitted, it is called "gray goods." Because of all the industrial processes this fabric has been through, the gray goods are dirty and still not ready to make into clothing. The fabric is rough and unappealing to the touch and to the eye. At this stage of production, many hands and many machines have touched it. And yet, more steps and more machines are still to come.

Depending on the type of clothing the gray goods are for, they are sent off to another factory for more treatments. These treatments can make the fabric softer to the touch, stain-resistant, or waterproof. Treatments can even add insect repellent to fabric. The finishing processes are separate from the dyeing or printing of the fabric.

Creating textiles for clothing is a complex, multistep process. Who are the people behind the innovations that make this process possible?

HELP WANTED

From the science necessary to grow cotton that uses fewer pesticides, to the chemistry required to develop new synthetic fibers, to the engineering behind the many machines used to change fiber into fabric, scientists and engineers play an important part in the process. They need to be analytical to figure out solutions to problems or to come up with new, innovative processes or materials. They need to be creative so they can take their thinking beyond the obvious. Of course, they also need to be technologically savvy to create machinery to complete a variety of tasks. Two jobs that require this multifaceted skill set are textile designers and textile engineers.

Today, much of the textile manufacturing for clothes sold in the United States is outsourced. As of 2018, China was the top producer and exporter of textiles in the world.

Textile designers come up with the designs and patterns that you see on fabrics, clothing, and even home goods. The designers have a far-reaching and deep knowledge of the wide variety of textiles available to work with, along with a firm grasp of the design and manufacturing processes. They also need to understand their customers as well as current trends driving the market.

Fabrics come in all different colors and designs.

Say that you are a textile designer working for a company that makes casual wear for teens. You are asked to design a pattern to be printed on a new line of summer dresses.

FELTING

Felting is a less common, nonwoven way of creating textiles. Woolen fibers are dampened and tangled to form a dense, mat-like cloth and then heated, causing the fibers to shrink tightly together. Felted fabric is mainly used for industrial purposes, such as padding and insulation.

Industrial textile factories operate much differently than a textile artisan's workshop.

Your first task is to find just the right fabric. To do this, you need to understand the characteristics of various fabrics. Consider fiber types, yarn size, and what kind of finishes will be applied to the fabric.

The next step is designing the pattern for the fabric. This is when you think about what kinds of dyes go best with the type of fabric you want to use and how those dyes or designs will be printed onto the fabric. When you finally begin to create the design, you will probably do it using the latest computer assisted design (CAD) program. As you can see, a lot of knowledge and decision making goes into a design found on a single piece of clothing.

Another important job in the textile industry is the textile engineer. These engineers design the machines required for each step of the manufacturing process. They might invent machines that conserve energy or come up with processes that create less pollution.

Some textile engineers do research and development to think of new products, which will eventually require new methods and machines.

Plus, since the textile industry is much bigger than just fabric, textile engineers often work outside of the fashion industry. For instance, textile engineers work with NASA to create new materials to use in space, with the medical industry to come up with products for operating rooms, and in many other industrial and technical fields where textiles are commonly found.

NATURE KNOWS BEST

Textile engineers often find ideas for innovative new fabrics in nature. The idea for Velcro came about in 1941 when an engineer and entrepreneur named George de Mestral (1907–1990) noticed that burrs got stuck to his clothing. Wondering why this happened, he took a closer look under a microscope and noticed that the small hooks on the burr attached exceedingly well to the loops of his clothing. He copied this concept in the design of Velcro.

Another example of biomimicry is Speedo's creation of a swimming suit that would help swimmers go even faster. Scientists at London's Natural History Museum in England, studied sharks and found that a pattern of tiny "teeth" on a shark's skin reduces drag. Engineers duplicated this pattern on Speedo's Fastskin swimsuits.

Have you seen any other examples of biomimicry in this chapter?

To see textile manufacturing in action, as well as preview the process of dyeing and finishing fabric, check out this video.

Why are textile engineers such an important part of the fashion industry?

how made fabric

FABRIC FACT

Feeling the need to send a friend a hug? You can if you both own the hug dress! Made with special sensors that detect when the wearer hugs themself, that hug can be transmitted via Bluetooth to another person wearing a hug dress.

BAMBOO FABRIC

Fiber obtained from the cellulose in the pulp of the bamboo plant produces bamboo fabric that is gaining in popularity. Since it is a grass, bamboo grows back quickly once it is harvested—it doesn't even have to be replanted. It requires half the amount of land and significantly less water to grow than cotton and doesn't need toxic pesticides. Lyocell is another type of bamboo fabric that is eco-friendly. Keep your eyes out for bamboo fashion!

INNOVATIVE TRENDS

As technology and science continue to advance and modern lifestyles and activities continue to change, new textiles and new ways of manufacturing them are being invented. Smart textiles fall into this category.

What are smart textiles? They are fabrics that have computer-based technology woven into them. These textiles use some of the same digital communication technology found in smartphones!

They not only perceive changes in the environment, they can respond accordingly. They may have the ability to regulate body temperature, protect the wearer against changing weather, or even light up or change color. For example, you might someday wear a coat that heats up when you get cold, a shirt that adjusts its breathability according to your body temperature when you are jogging, or a dress that changes color to the beat of the music.

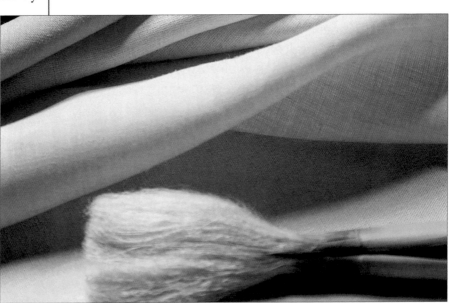

Bamboo is an environmentally friendly material used to make textiles.

Sustainable fabric is another trend that is gaining momentum in the fashion industry.

Sustainable fabrics are made from eco-friendly resources and manufactured in a way that doesn't pollute the environment. For instance, textile engineers and scientists who are on the lookout for environmentally friendly resources are experimenting with new sources for fiber, including coffee grounds and cellulose from banana trees.

Another aspect of sustainability is finding ways to produce textiles in more environmentally sound ways. For example, blue-jean makers are coming up with manufacturing methods that use less water. They are also using natural dyes instead of toxic chemicals that can find their way into nearby streams and waterways.

Finally, recycling used plastic bottles into textiles is another innovation that is good for the environment and makes sense economically. In fact, you might not even be aware how many of the clothes in your closet are created with synthetic textiles made this way. Fleece jackets, yoga pants, and quick-drying swimwear can be the product of recycled plastics.

Now that we know how fabrics are made, let's take a look at one of the first things many people notice about your clothes—the color!

What happens when fashion goes out of date—way, way out of date? Trained textile conservators take over, working to preserve ancient textiles and make them available for scientists and museum visitors to learn about the culture and technology of ancient times.

Learn about the work of textile conservationists here.

Fabric Fashion FIT

KEY QUESTIONS

- **What are the two categories of fibers? How are they different from each other? How is each type of fiber turned into yarn?**
- **What are the two ways yarn is turned into fabric?**
- **Do you know anyone who knits or weaves or crochets? How is what they do different from what happens in a textile factory?**

TEXT TO WORLD

Have you ever seen sheep? What does their wool look like? What does the wool do for the sheep that makes it a nice material for clothing?

Ideas for Supplies ▼

- heavy cardboard
- yarn in different colors
- large, blunt-tipped tapestry needle

VOCAB LAB

Write down what you think each word means. What root words can you find to help you? What does the context of the word tell you?

biomimicry, cellulose, fiber, filament, globalization, knitting, polymer, supply chain, and **sustainable**.

Compare your definitions with those of your friends or classmates. Did you all come up with the same meanings? Turn to the text and glossary if you need help.

WEAVE IT YOURSELF

Now it's your turn to create a loom. Yours will be more like an ancient loom than the industrial looms used in textile production today. As you weave, see if you come up with your own technological advances to make your weaving experience more efficient and effective. Innovate!

- **Create the frame for your loom.**

  - Cut a strong piece of cardboard into an 8-by-8-inch square.

  - Using a ruler, draw two lines across the width of the cardboard, each line a half inch from the bottom and top of the cardboard.

  - Across the width of the cardboard, along the bottom and top, draw small, evenly spaced lines. It is important that you have the same number of lines on both top and bottom.

  - Using scissors, cut each of those lines up to the straight line drawn across the width.

- **Attach warp threads to frame.**

  - Unwind, but don't cut, a length of yarn from a skein. Leaving a 5- or 6-inch tail, slip the yarn through the first cut at the bottom of the frame. Begin to tightly wrap the yarn continuously around the frame, going from bottom to top and anchoring the yarn in the cuts you made at each end. (Hint: It is a good idea to use a ball of yarn or a skein because you don't know exactly how much yarn this will take.)

  - When the frame is filled, cut the yarn leaving enough to tightly tie the tail of yarn from the beginning to the yarn at the end. This is now the back of your loom.

• **Begin weaving with weft yarn.**

- Cut a long piece of yarn and thread a large, blunt, tapestry needle. Tie yarn to the needle's eye.

- Begin weaving by threading yarn over one warp thread and then under the next one. Continue across all warp yarn. Once again, leave a tail of yarn at the beginning of the first row.

- Push the woven row down to the bottom of the loom and begin the next row. If you ended one row by going under the warp yarn you will begin the next row by going over it.

- Keep weaving in this way until the piece is complete or until you want to change thread colors.

- To change weft colors, simply leave a 2- or 3-inch tail of yarn of the old color at the end of a row and begin with a new color. When the piece is done, you can weave any tails into several rows along the back of the weaving.

- As you weave, don't forget to pay attention to changes that you make in order to make the process more efficient.

> To investigate more, try to weave in a pattern, figuring out a way to make it easier to separate the weft threads for each alternating row. Also, can you make a weaving out of material other than yarn, possibly recycling colorful plastic bags, ribbons, or strips of old clothing?

Meet Sydney Kidwell, a textile engineer. In this interview, you get a glimpse into different aspects of the job. She shares some of the difficulties she faced in school as well as some great advice she got when she was struggling with a hard class in college.

Learn more about Kidwell's work here.

Sydney Kidwell women STEM

TECHNOLOGY:
A DOUBLE-EDGED SWORD

Advancements brought about by science and engineering discoveries and innovation often come at a price. For this reason, technology is often seen as a double-edged sword. Because its introduction might solve social problems or make economic growth possible, it also often causes unexpected or unintended consequences.

Watch this PBS video titled *The African Americans: Many Rivers to Come/The Cotton Gin*, keeping in mind the idea of unintended consequences.

PBS classroom
cotton gin

- **In your science notebook, write your thoughts and answers to the following questions.**

  - Whose responsibility is it to think through and predict the possible negative consequences of positive technological advances?

  - Thinking back over what you learned in this chapter, can you name other negative consequences from advances in the textile industry?

> To investigate more, list some current scientific advancements beyond the textile industry. How about medical advances, space exploration, and new smart technology? Choose one and think about what unintended consequences might result from this advancement. Should scientific advancements be avoided when negative consequences are possible?

Chapter 2 ▶
The Chemistry of Color

SOME DAYS, YOU JUST WANT TO WEAR THE WHOLE RAINBOW.

How are science and engineering involved in coloring your clothing?

PEOPLE HAVE BEEN USING DYE TO MAKE COLORFUL CLOTHING FOR A VERY LONG TIME.

DYES COME FROM ALL SORTS OF WEIRD PLACES.

MOLLUSKS CAN PRODUCE A BEAUTIFUL SHADE OF PURPLE!

RED DYE ORIGINALLY CAME FROM A PLANT ROOT. THE BRAZILWOOD TREE CREATES A RANGE OF MOSTLY WARM COLORS.

NATURE IS SO WEIRD AND WONDERFUL!

From the impact on mood, looks, and the environment, color is a key part of fashion! Researchers are always working on new ways to make colorful fabrics while lessening the damage to our planet.

Imagine a world—or a closet—without color. Color is all around you, but how often do you really notice it? Most people take the richness and variety of color for granted. A crystal blue sky dappled with white clouds on a winter morning, an autumn tree lit up with orange and red leaves, and a summer garden exploding with pinks and purples and many shades of green—these are just a few of the luscious colors that nature offers up to those who take the time to notice.

Nature isn't the only place where you find color. A couch's woven geometric patterns look nice against splashes of bright color on the curtains and rug. A multicolor vase glistens on a black metal coffee table and a fire pops and crackles in a cream-colored cement fireplace. While the wide variety of colors in nature appears without human help, everything manmade has color added to it.

These colors are no accident. Someone carefully selected, created, and applied color to the object.

THE SCIENCE OF COLOR

Being able to choose the perfect color or color combination is one important key to a designer's success. Understanding the power of color to influence feelings, knowing what colors work best together, and recognizing how color interacts with light are factors that designers must consider from the very beginning of the design process. This is true whether they are working with materials for clothing, a kitchen, an office building, or a train station.

It's a knowledge that comes from studying the science behind color, or color theory.

How do we see color in the first place? It works like this. Light travels in waves and contains all colors. When light hits an object, that object absorbs all the colors in the spectrum except its own color, which is reflected to your eyes. This is where the sensation of color is formed.

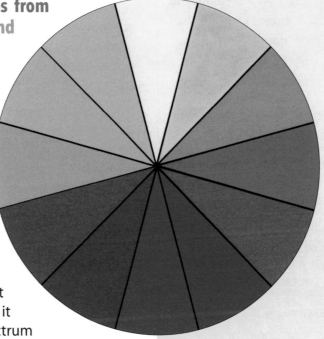

Color wheel

So, if the chair you are looking at is blue, when light hits the chair it absorbs all the colors in the spectrum except blue, which bounces back to your eyes. That is the color you see. The less light there is, the less color you see. This is another fact that designers need to account for when creating a piece of clothing. The amount of light changes how you perceive the color of a fabric.

Try a light experiment for yourself. Go into your room and make note of the colors you see. Now, dim the lights or pull down the shades. Do the colors look different? Did all the colors change in the same way? How would knowing this affect which colors you might choose when designing clothing?

How do our eyes and brains process primary and secondary colors differently? It all has to do with what's going on inside our eyes, not outside.

Learn more in this video!

TED-ED Colm Kelleher

The modern understanding of light was first introduced by Isaac Newton (1642–1726). In 1672, by shining a ray of light through a prism, he discovered that light is made up of a rainbow, or spectrum, of colors. Red is on one side of the spectrum and violet is on the other.

Newton joined the ends of the spectrum together, creating what we now know as the color wheel. He broke down the colors of the spectrum into primary colors (red, blue, yellow) and secondary colors (violet, green, orange). Secondary colors come from mixing primary colors together.

One hundred years later, the writer and philosopher Johann Wolfgang Goethe (1749–1832) began studying the psychological effects of color, noticing that yellow produces a warming effect, while blue "feels" cool. Goethe created a color wheel that assigned an emotional response to each color.

This color research from Newton and Goethe laid the foundation for modern color theory, which explains and explores how colors, light, and emotion work together.

FABRIC FACT

⟨⟩⟨⟩⟨⟩⟨⟩⟨⟩⟨⟩⟨⟩⟨⟩⟨⟩⟨⟩⟨⟩

Check out some color words!

Hue: the 12 purest and brightest colors, also the colors on a basic color wheel.

Value: the degree of lightness or darkness of a color.

Intensity: the purity of the color and the degree to which it is free of weakening forces, such as the addition of white or black.

Primary colors: the colors red, yellow, and blue that, when mixed, create all the other colors.

Secondary colors: the colors violet, orange, and green that are made by mixing two primary colors.

Tertiary colors: the colors created when mixing a primary color with a secondary color.

Complementary colors: opposites on the color wheel (blue/orange, red/green, yellow/violet).

Artists and designers use color theory as they create designs that are both aesthetically pleasing and psychologically appealing.

Have you ever heard the expression "green with envy"? How do you feel when you are "feeling blue"? If you are drawing a cartoon of someone who is angry, what color might you make their face? Advertisers, artists, and designers use this unspoken, common knowledge when they create products.

For designers, understanding the color wheel helps them know which colors complement each other and which colors clash. It helps designers know when to use warm colors in their designs and when cool colors would be more appropriate. They can choose colors that match different seasons and different activities.

The type of mollusk once used to make purple dye

Credit: H. Crisp (CC BY 3.0)

A HISTORY OF COLOR IN CLOTHING

Humans have been using dye to add color to their wardrobes since at least 2600 BCE, and probably long before. The earliest dyes came from three sources. The plants indigo and woad both produced a blue hue, while a type of mollusk, called murex, produced a highly desirable and expensive shade of purple.

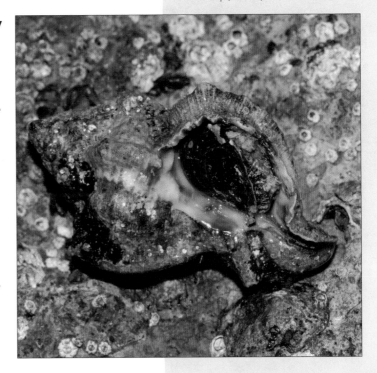

As time passed, people discovered new sources for dye. Red dye appeared on the scene around the tenth century and came from the roots of the madder plant. In the 1200s, the weld plant added yellow to the color palette, while the early 1300s brought the discovery that the Brazilwood tree created coral, red, pink, and purple. By the 1500s, insects became a source of dye when the Mayans started using cochineal insects to create crimson.

For centuries, people only used the plants, and therefore the colors, available to them locally to create their dyes.

Look at the different plants used to create dyes.

Credit: Brian Snelson (CC BY 2.0)

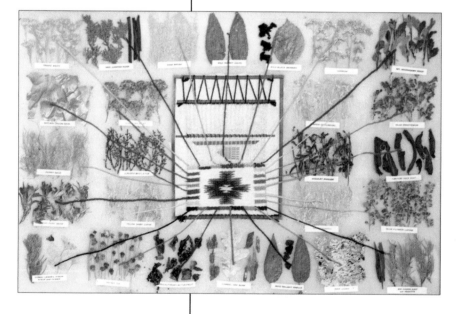

During the 1500s, entrepreneurs in France, Germany, and the Netherlands began raising these plants as cash crops to sell farther afield.

Everything changed in 1856. William Henry Perkin, an 18-year-old chemist studying at the Royal College of Science, was trying to come up with a synthetic version of a popular malaria-fighting drug. His experiment failed but, in the process, he accidentally discovered the first synthetic dye. From that time, synthetic dyes began to replace the natural plant- and insect-based dyes.

COLORING BETWEEN THE LINES

Color is added to unfinished textiles, or gray goods, through two methods. One is coloring with natural or synthetic pigments, and the other is using dyes.

Most dyes used for clothing are synthetic, made from coal tar or petroleum-based products.

Pigments, sometimes referred to as pigment dyes, are made of insoluble color particles—meaning they do not dissolve in water. A chemical binding agent, which works like glue, attaches the pigment particles to the fiber.

Coloring fabric with pigments is quick, simple, and economical. Pigments come in a wide range of color and, because the color particles are bound to the outside of the fabric, they can be used on almost any fabric.

An advantage of coloring fabric with pigment is that the process does not use much water. A disadvantage is that the color only attaches to the outside of the fabric, so the color might fade after several washings. Have you ever had this happen to a favorite shirt? You can think of a pigment-dyed textile like an apple, where the color is only on the outside.

FABRIC FACT
◇◇◇◇◇◇◇◇◇◇◇◇◇◇◇◇◇◇◇◇◇◇◇◇◇

William Henry Perkin knew the value of his accidental discovery of synthetic dye. He dropped out of school in 1857 and, with the financial backing of his father, set up the world's first industrial chemical plant in Greenford Green, England. Can you think of other inventions that were the result of a mistake?

The Stockholm Papyrus was a collection of dyeing recipes written sometime between 300 and 400 CE. Here is the recipe for dyeing wool purple: "Boil asphodel and natron, put the wool in it 8 drachmas at a time and rinse it out. Then take and bruise 1 mina of grape skins, mix these with vinegar and let stand 6 hours. Then boil the mixture and put the wool in." You can read more of the recipes at this website.

How are these instructions different from those you might find in dyeing instructions today?

recipes Stockholm Papyrus

Pigment comes in liquid or paste form. Both can be used to add color to textiles.

Dyeing is another way of adding color to fabric. It is generally done using a liquid solution that contains the dye and other specially selected chemicals. The textile is completely saturated in the dye mixture, and the dyes penetrate the fabric fibers, where they bond chemically.

Dyeing permanently changes the color of the fabric all the way through. The color of a dyed fabric is like a carrot, all one color.

The dye chemist has a wide range of color to work with. The human eye can see around 350,000 colors.

FABRIC FACT

Coal tar is a thick, dark liquid that comes from coal, while petroleum products are made from crude oil. Coal and crude oil are fossil fuels formed deep in the earth from deposits of ancient animal and marine organisms. Both are a nonrenewable energy source, and neither is biodegradable.

Dyes can be applied to fiber, yarn, finished textiles, or even completed garments. Dyes have much greater color strength than pigments. A little dye can color large amounts of fabric, whereas much more pigment would be required to color the same amount of fabric.

THE SCIENCE BEHIND COLORING WITH DYE

Adding color to fabric might seem simple. Just mix up the dye, add water and fabric, and, voilà, instant color. The truth is, getting that color into your clothing is quite an involved process.

The scientists and engineers who create both the commercial dyes and the manufacturing processes required to get the dye into the fabric have much to consider. Fiber chemistry plays an important role. Each textile has a unique dyeing flow chart, requiring different chemicals and different processes for the material to successfully receive and hold the color.

For the color to be permanent and uniform, the chemistry of the dye and that of the fiber must match.

Natural dyes
Credit: USAG-Humphreys (CC BY 2.0)

Plus, if other finishes are being added to the textile, such as waterproofing, the chemist must consider these finishes along with environmental complications that might affect the product. Exposure to sunlight and weather can also affect the material.

Scientists must also understand how a product is to be used. For example, a dye created to color clothing would not be used for curtains because curtain dyes need to stay colorfast when exposed to daily sunlight. Many pieces of clothing spend far more time indoors, out of the sun's brilliance.

Dyeing machines come in all shapes and sizes. In general, they contain a barrel-like vessel big enough to hold large quantities of the dye. Traditionally, a winch reel would draw the fabric through the dyebath. New technologies are now replacing the traditional ones. One innovation uses pressurized jets to apply the dye. This saves water and energy.

Have you ever tie-dyed a T-shirt?

THE SCIENCE BEHIND COLORING WITH PRINTING

Printing is the process for adding color designs to fabrics. If a design or pattern is not woven into the fabric, it is probably printed on it. While dyeing adds color to an entire piece of fabric, printing adds color to localized areas to create patterns. Chemically bonded to the fabric, the color does not fade with repeated washing.

Patterns and designs are possible with printing that cannot be achieved any other way. The color for printing comes from pigments or dyes and is applied with special machines. Often, more than one color is applied in a step-by-step process.

As with dyeing, creating colors for textile printing is both an art and a science. It requires chemical knowledge to make sure the dye or pigment is right for the fabric, the pattern, and the function of the clothing. It also requires extensive knowledge of the machines and technology being used to create a specific print, because different machines have different requirements. Plus, the color must be specifically formulated to withstand the demands of wear and tear created by this multistep process.

As with dyeing, many methods of printing are possible. The ultimate decision of which one to use depends on the pattern, the type of color being used, the fabric weight, and, of course, cost.

Digital textile printing uses digital inkjet printing technology. As with all textile designs, the digitally printed fabric begins with artists coming up with a design. Using a graphic design program such as Adobe Illustrator, they can create and format the design, store it, and transfer it without losing any details. Some people choose to create the design by hand and then convert it to a digital format.

Look at this video to find out how digital textile printing is done!

How can you relate this technological method to the hand method used by today's artisans and people in the past?

Textile Vlog
printing tech

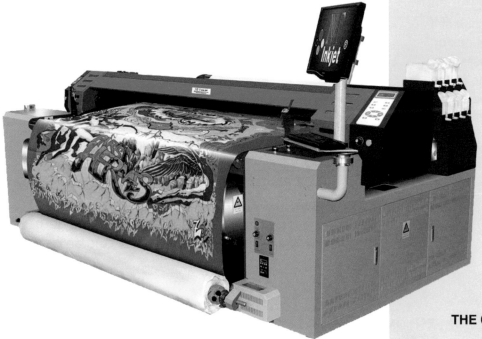

Digital textile printing

Once the design is created, it is ready to be transferred to the fabric, which has already been treated with special chemical solutions that allow it to accept and absorb the dye. Using inkjet technology, the fabric is fed through the printer, where dye cartridges release the dye, much like the ink cartridges do on your printer at home or school. After the design is printed, it is treated with a fixing agent that ensures the design is permanent and will not fade away.

Screen printing is commonly used to print on clothing. This is when a fine mesh screen with a picture or pattern is placed on the fabric and an operator or machine moves a squeegee or blade across the screen, filling in the open parts of the mesh with ink. First invented in China between 960 and 1279, this process was called silk screening because it was done on silk.

Block printing is another printing technique, dating back to the ancient civilizations of India, Egypt, China, and Assyria. In this method, a design is carved onto a wooden or metal block. The dye is applied to the block, which is then pressed onto the fabric's surface.

THE ENVIRONMENTAL IMPACT

The brightly colored clothing you wear comes at a price to the environment. An estimated 20 percent of global water pollution is linked to the textile dyeing process. Most of the dyes used in commercial dyeing are synthetic and are made using non-biodegradable, petroleum-based colorants.

FABRIC FACT

A benefit of digital printing is the ability to do "on demand" shorter print runs, potentially meaning less waste.

As scientists look for greener ways to make dye, many clothing companies are seeking innovative solutions. Read about some of the newest solutions.

Can you think of other inventions or new processes that might help the fashion industry land on the side of planet Earth?

PreScouter greener textiles

During the dyeing process, the dye is dissolved in a water solution. Although most of that dye is absorbed into the fibers, 10 to 15 percent of the dye is not. That water, loaded with chemicals, becomes wastewater. Since much of the industry's dyeing takes places in developing countries that don't have strict laws and regulations for environmentally safe ways to clean and handle that wastewater, much of it is dumped directly into streams and waterways.

Another environmental negative of the dyeing process is that it requires lots and lots of water.

Dyeing an average T-shirt uses an estimated 4 to 5 gallons of water! Much of that water is absorbed into the fabric, which means that it is no longer part of the water cycle. That water will never again be available for human use, such as drinking, cooking, bathing, or producing energy.

When chemicals are dumped into local waterways, they pollute the water, negatively affecting the local ecosystems. Plus, local citizens often use this water for drinking, causing health issues.

This river in Bangladesh is polluted from nearby mills that dump chemical waste into the water.

CLEAN COLOR

As you've already read, dyeing textiles is a dirty business requiring massive amounts of water and synthetic dyes. Scientists and engineers are creating innovative technologies to make dyeing clothing more sustainable.

Here are a few of the newest solutions.

CEN ACS
sustainable

Luckily, dye and clothing manufacturers are slowly beginning to make changes. Some dyeing and clothing companies are taking active roles in cleaning up the dyeing process. Scientists continue to work on developing cleaner dyes, such as those that come from natural sources. Engineers are working on technologies to make the process of adding color to textiles cleaner and greener. Digital printing is one such technology.

As consumers, we have a responsibility as well. We need to learn how our clothing is created. Even though eco-friendly clothing is more expensive, we need to support those companies that are working to be part of the solution instead of part of the problem.

Now that we know how our clothes gain color, let's take a look at the whole outfit—how do designers decide what characteristics clothing will have and what it will actually look like? We'll learn more in the next chapter.

KEY QUESTIONS

- **What is your favorite color? What do certain colors make you feel? Do you think this is unique to every person, or do colors have a universal mood adjuster?**

- **How do designers use color theory in their design process?**

- **What are some things a dyer might need to consider to create the best dye for a fabric?**

- **How does dyeing affect the environment? Why is it important to look for new ways of coloring textiles without negative repercussions?**

TEXT TO WORLD

Can you think of ways you might be able to keep wearing the vibrant colors you love without hurting the environment?

Inquire & Investigate

COLORFUL CHROMATOGRAPHY

Chromatography is a way to analyze complex mixtures. It works by passing them through a solvent that separates them into their components. Try this colorful demonstration to see how water works as a solvent to separate the components of different kinds of ink.

- **Cut a paper towel into a long strip.** Draw a pencil line across the strip about 1 inch from the bottom.

- **Along the line, make three dots with different colored markers.** The dots should have a generous amount of ink and should be evenly spaced.

- **Clip the top of the strip to a pencil and balance the pencil over the top of a glass so the strip is hanging down.** It should not touch the bottom or sides of the glass.

- **Fill the glass with enough water to touch the bottom of the strip.** The water should not touch the ink.

- **Leave the paper towel in the glass for at least 10 minutes.** Watch what happens!

To investigate more, cut out 2-inch circles of paper towels or use the middle of a white coffee filter. Using your washable markers, decorate the circles. Placing each decorated circle on a plate, use a dropper and slowly saturate them with water. Instant art!

VOCAB LAB

Write down what you think each word means. What root words can you find to help you? What does the context of the word tell you?

aesthetic, **color theory**, **complement**, **dye**, **pigment**, **saturate**, and **wastewater**.

Compare your definitions with those of your friends or classmates. Did you all come up with the same meanings? Turn to the text and glossary if you need help.

DYE IT YOURSELF

Albert Einstein said, "The only source of knowledge is experience." Now that you've read all about the dyeing process, it's your turn to experience some of that process yourself.

- **Mix one part vinegar to four parts water in the pot.** This is called a fixative. Put the fabric in the fixative, bring it to a boil, and then let it simmer for an hour. After it cools, pour the mixture into a sieve set in the sink and thoroughly rinse with cool water.

- **To make the dye, combine one type of plant material in a pot with water.** The more plant product you use, the more color you will get. The more water you use, the more diluted the color will be. You might start with about a cup of plant material and several cups of water.

- **Bring your pot to a boil and then simmer for more than an hour.** After the mixture cools, strain all of the plant material from the dye.

- **Add the fabric to the dye, making sure it is completely submerged.** Again, bring it to a boil and let it simmer for at least an hour. Turn off the heat and let it soak overnight.

- **Remove the fabric from the dye and rinse with cold water.** To seal in the color, put the fabric in the dryer and then press with an iron.

> To investigate more, continue to try different plant-based materials to create colors you like. Keep track of your dye "recipes" so you can repeat them if you like the results!

Chapter 3 ▶
The Fundamentals of Design

FASHION CREATES LOTS OF DIFFERENT AND INTERESTING FIELDS OF WORK!

How do science and engineering impact or influence fashion design?

THE WAY CLOTHING IS CREATED AND DISTRIBUTED HAS CHANGED DRASTICALLY WITH NEW TECHNOLOGY.

CLOTHING WENT FROM BEING 100-PERCENT HANDSEWN TO BEING PUT TOGETHER BY AUTOMATED SEWING MACHINES.

NOW, WE CAN MAKE CLOTHING MORE QUICKLY AND EASILY.

DESIGN
MARKETING PRODUCTION
DISTRIBUTION
RETAIL

THAT MEANS DESIGNERS HAVE A LOT MORE "MATERIAL" TO WORK WITH!

The world of fashion would be pretty boring without the science and engineering that drives innovation and results in new materials, new designs, new functionality, and new ways of dealing with old clothes!

When you walk through your favorite clothing store or browse online and see next season's fashions on display, do you ever wonder how those fashions got there? Who decides on the latest fashion trends? Is it the designer, the retailer, or the consumer?

Why does one type of fashion take off and another barely sell? How does the design that starts in a creator's head turn into a real piece of clothing in a store? Is fashion design a learned skill or a talent you are born with?

All these questions have to do with the part of the fashion industry that is responsible for design. Creative, artistic fashion designers are at the epicenter of the trillion-dollar global fashion industry. Their work and vision are necessary to get those new designs to you.

But, as you will see in this chapter, even in the design phase, science, engineering, and technology play critical roles.

FITTING INTO THE DESIGN PROCESS

Fashion design begins with a sketchbook and an eye for inspiration. Sounds easy at first, until you ask yourself, where do ideas come from? And how does the spark of an idea turn into the spring collection of fashion on display in your local department store?

FABRIC FACT

Haute couture, or high fashion, is expensive, exclusive, high-end fashion that is made and custom fitted for individual clients. Ready-to-wear, or prêt-à-porter, clothing is factory-made in standard sizes. Fast fashion is often poorly made, inexpensive clothing that is rapidly produced by a mass market retailer in response to ever-changing fashion trends.

Students in fashion school learn the design process, which is a recommended set of steps a designer follows to take them from inspiration to finished product.

Designers start by putting the business of fashion first as they work to fully understand how best to meet the needs of the clients they have in mind. What do consumers want? How much do they want to spend? How does that compare to what the materials will cost? When must the new fashion line be available? Also, designing for teen consumers involves different requirements than designing for adults. Having this information before beginning the design process shapes all the design decisions.

Once a designer has defined the constraints, or limits, for the design, they are ready to start the process of designing. This usually begins with a search for inspiration. Where do you look for inspiration when you're creating something?

Vintage fashion

THE FUNDAMENTALS OF DESIGN

Sergio Hudson designed not one, but two outfits for the January 2021 U.S. presidential inauguration. One was worn by former First Lady Michelle Obama and the other by Vice President Kamala Harris. Hudson says that the industry has to be willing to invest in Black designers.

Inspiration can be an individual thing, but many designers look at clothing styles from the past, browse clothing from other cultures, shop in vintage stores, and watch old movies. Inspiration might also be sparked by an unusual color combination in a painting at a museum. Even a feeling conjured up from visiting an old mansion or a ski lodge can provide that flash of insight that innovation is often based on.

The internet can be a useful tool when a designer is looking for inspiration. Apps such as Pinterest and Instagram can be a way to see what kinds of styles are trending. Designers can look at photo archives in museums, research the latest trends in textiles, and even access photos or images from distant destinations.

As designers collect and save the images and colors and textures that inspire them in a real or virtual sketchbook, they look for a theme and a feeling, or mood. The mood or theme can tie together all their garments in a collection.

Once a designer has decided on the theme, they often create a kind of inspiration board to bring all the relevant images, words, colors, and textures together in one place. Those images are a useful reference during the actual design process.

Some designers also create a mood board that sets the emotional feeling of a collection as well as the style and the colors dictated by that feeling.

FABRIC FACT

Search "images of fashion theme boards" to get an idea how different designers put together their inspirations. What kinds of things jump out at you? Do you see any common themes?

Before technology, these boards were just large posters, but now they can be digital and include sound and movement. Designers use these mood boards to present their vision to others, including retailers.

But inspiration is not design. Eventually, the design of the clothing must begin. Again, different designers have different ways of starting this process. Some go old school with the traditional pencil and paper, while other use the latest CAD tools.

A fashion design

Once the design is created, the work of making it into a reality begins. At this point, a pattern for each piece of clothing is created and then used to cut and sew a prototype. This rough draft of the design is fitted on a dressform, where the designer alters and refines it until the garment is just what they had envisioned. The final design is saved on a computer.

THE HOUSE OF WORTH

Charles Frederick Worth (1825–1895) is often referred to as the father of haute couture. Before Worth, dressmakers made clothing and royalty dictated fashion trends. In 1845, Worth, a tailor, left London, England, for Paris, France, and set up his own tailor's shop for women. He was the first designer to tell customers what to wear instead of simply creating what they demanded. His shop became the House of Worth, and he was the first fashion designer recognized by name.

A dressform allows the designer to refit and adjust pieces without worrying about needing another person, at least at the beginning of the process. Eventually, designers use a real person, called a fit model, to see how the piece works.

From there, the design is passed electronically to manufacturers, along with precise measurements for the pattern for the clothing as well as detailed instructions for assembling the garment. But many, many more designs are created than make it through the manufacturing process and end up in stores near you!

THE TECHNOLOGY OF DESIGN

The designer's creativity and artistry is the heart of the fashion design process. Technology, however, has made it a lot easier for that creativity and artistry to get to the final version of a design.

CAD programs were originally developed to design the precision machinery needed in manufacturing. Those machines must precisely cut, grind, shape, mold, or melt material. As time passed, the ability to make specific blueprints with CAD allowed this technology to be applied in other ways, such as fashion design.

In the fashion industry, designers can use CAD software at all stages of the design process, from first sketches to prototypes to finished designs complete with measurements.

Designers can experiment with color and different fabrics and easily make changes, all on a computer. When ready, those two-dimensional designs can be viewed in three dimensions, allowing the designer to see how the garment looks on a virtual model. With all this work being done on the computer, much of the time-consuming fine-tuning of the design process can be accomplished before sewing the prototypes, saving time and money.

In today's rush for fast fashion, when retailers want to stock the latest trending fashions as quickly as possible, the use of CAD saves time and helps make money. In addition, with the availability of cloud-based CAD software, designers can more easily share ideas and collaborate.

Designers can also use CAD software to create patterns in a variety of sizes through a process called grading, as well as create and share the technical information required for manufacturing. This is especially important when the manufacturing takes place in a country far away from where the design is taking place. Today, all students enrolled in fashion design programs learn to use CAD software.

DATA AND DESIGN

One important partnership in the fashion industry is the one between the design team and data scientists. Information from data science influences what designers design as well as how, where, and even for how long a piece of clothing is sold.

Check out this quick video on the history of CAD.

How might the fashion industry be different if CAD was never developed? Are there any drawbacks to using CAD?

walk through history CAD

Clothes need to sell so everyone in the industry stays in business!

GENDER NEUTRAL

English singer and actor Harry Styles (1994–) appeared on the December 2020 of *Vogue* wearing a dress and pearls. This is another in a long line of signs that the fashion world is embracing the idea of clothing for all genders. Gender-neutral clothing is not designed to show off a woman's figure or a man's muscles and is not labeled as clothing for a man or a woman. Many designer brands are beginning to promote this type of clothing and there are even gender-neutral stores opening up. Turns out, people like clothes that fit their mood, personality, and tastes, no matter their gender.

But what is data science? It's a multidisciplinary field consisting of statistics, data engineering, software analysis, and more. Teams of experts in these fields gather data from a wide variety of sources. Using scientific, statistical, and mathematical processes, they analyze data to gain knowledge and insights to answer specific questions or address specific problems.

Data science is not a new field, and the fashion industry has used data science companies to help designers capitalize on fashion and color trends in the past.

However, thanks to the recent explosion of technology, the type of data that is now being gathered is changing. Huge amounts of data are now available from social media, mobile devices, computers, and tablets. In addition, data scientists might collect data on what is trending on Instagram, what celebrities are wearing, how people shop, and what they buy online.

A fashion designer might consult with data scientists prior to designing to learn about upcoming trends in clothing styles and color. This information can highlight different style trends for different age groups, genders, or even geographic areas of the country or the world. This is valuable information for the designer. Although the act of designing is a creative one, that creativity is no good unless the results of those designs—the clothes—sell well.

The data provided by data scientists is just another tool for designers to use. Data scientists do not tell designers how or what to design. But the information and insights that data science provides can guide the designer's decisions. Ultimately, the final design decisions belong to the designer.

JUST ADD COLOR

As we discussed in the last chapter, color is one of the most important ingredients in a successful design. Research tells us that a person's decision whether to buy a certain product happens in the first 90 seconds—and 90 percent of that choice is based on color.

Obviously, fashion designers are under a lot of pressure to get the color decision right. Luckily, they have several tools available to help them make this critical decision.

Data scientists help by providing information about colors that are trending, while CAD apps allow the designer to easily see how different color choices affect the balance and beauty of a design. The early work done with inspiration and mood boards also helps the designer pick colors that tie into the overall story or theme of the design collection.

Seasonal collections can help designers limit their choices because of different palettes tied to the feeling, holidays, and mood of each season. For example, when designers work on the fall season, the colors will be different from those for spring clothing.

What colors do you often see people wearing during the winter season? Does this depend on where you live?

Data scientists also provide valuable information to retailers, letting them know which designs customers are most likely to purchase, what colors and sizes are most likely to sell, and even the best price for each item.

The Pantone Color System is a standardized system of 2,100 colors that helps designers choose colors. It is also a numerical recipe for that color so manufacturers can ensure the correct shade is used.

Another thing that helps with color choice is that many clothing brands have already defined their own color story and designers must work within those guidelines. For example, the color story of a brand marketed at older, conservative men might include dark, serious colors, while the color story of a brand aimed at young men might have brighter, lighter colors.

The language of color is fluid because meanings change through time. For instance, although pink is now identified as a color for girls, up until the beginning of the twentieth century, pink was almost exclusively a color used and associated with little boys. Why do you think trends like this change? What might that say about the styles that are popular today?

The use of color is a critical choice in fashion design. Luckily, designers have scientific research and all sorts of technology to help them make the perfect color choice for each piece of clothing. They also have creative instinct!

TEXT TO WORLD

If you were to design a pair of pants that were comfortable, good looking, and easy to care for, what are some of the materials and methods you'd use?

FASHION MANUFACTURING

Once a design is finalized and approved, the next step is to put it into production. Although most of the clothing sold in the United States is designed in the United States, the manufacturing is often outsourced to other countries, where labor is cheaper. These countries include China, Bangladesh, Vietnam, and India.

The manufacturing process includes creating the patterns for different sizes, cutting the fabric, sewing it, and preparing it for shipment. Finally, the garment is distributed to retailers and, ideally, winds up in the hands of consumers.

As in many other industries, the fashion industry sees customers demand faster turnaround times for their clothing. Sewing robots, or sewbots, are one innovation that has arisen to try to help people in the industry meet demand.

Traditionally, sewing has been done by hand, step-by-step, in an assembly line of sewers with sewing machines. Handling fabric is unpredictable because of its highly flexible nature, so creating automated machines to sew garments has always been difficult. With the invention of the sewbot, however, more manufacturing companies are beginning to experiment with this type of automation.

Beyond clothing, fashion encompasses the accessories we wear and carry, such as backpacks, water bottles, jewelry, and more! Let's learn the science behind accessories in the next chapter.

KEY QUESTIONS

- Have you ever designed or invented a prototype or a new way of doing something? What steps did you take?

- Why is data science important to the fashion industry? In what other industries does it play a large role?

- What might the fashion industry be like without CAD?

FABRIC FACT

The nerve endings in human fingers give us the ability to feel when fabric is not flat before it goes under the sewing needle, something we have not yet been able to reproduce in sewbots. That's part of the reason it is still experimental.

Check out a sewing robot in action in this video!

Do you think artistry and robotics can work together to produce clothing that is both beautiful and efficiently made?

interesting engineering
sewing robot

DECONSTRUCTING THE SEWING ROBOT

A robot is a machine created to perform work and tasks previously done by people. Sewing robots are just beginning to be used in the fashion industry, and even a quick look shows that the engineering required to create one is quite complex! In this activity, you will deconstruct the work done by a sewing robot to get an idea of what types of challenges the engineer had to address when designing this technology.

• **Take another look at the short video of a sewing robot in action.** As you watch, name and describe some of the tasks that you see the robot accomplish.

  • What problems did the engineer need to overcome for the sewbot to successfully complete each task you identified?

  • How did the engineer handle those problems? Try and talk through the video, naming the challenges and offering up solutions to them.

To investigate more, think of a simple, one- or two-step manual task and consider how to automate that task. First, list the movements and abilities required to do each step. Second, list the constraints or problems that come up when thinking about automating that step. Brainstorm some possible solutions that might work.

CLOTHING MANUFACTURING FLOW CHART

You now know the basics about how a piece of clothing goes through many steps in many places on its journey into existence—from raw material to becoming a piece of fabric to being dyed or printed to being cut and sewed into a piece of clothing to sitting on a department store shelf to finally being brought home to be worn by you. Let's organize that information.

- **Choose your favorite piece of clothing.** Look at the tag that describes its fiber content and look up the manufacturer to figure out where the raw materials for that piece of clothing might have come from and where it was made.

- **On a large piece of paper, create a visual flow chart of each step in your clothing's journey.** Start with the raw materials and end with the finished product.

- **Add at least one significant bit of science and engineering knowledge required for each step.** What is something that made that step a possibility?

To investigate more, choose one of the pieces of science or engineering knowledge and research job possibilities in that field. What kind of education do you need? What skills does that job require? Can that job be done anywhere in the world? How much money do people make on average at that job?

VOCAB LAB

Write down what you think each word means. What root words can you find to help you? What does the context of the word tell you?

collaborate, **data scientist**, **designer**, **epicenter**, **palette**, **sewbot**, **theme**, and **trend**.

Compare your definitions with those of your friends or classmates. Did you all come up with the same meanings? Turn to the text and glossary if you need help.

DESIGN CREATIVITY

What are the stereotypes that you have about engineers? What are the stereotypes you have about fashion designers? Both engineers and fashion designers use a design process to create. However, people often look at the two professions very differently in terms of creativity. This activity will give you a chance to check out this thinking.

"Ah, the creative process is the same secret in science as in art. They are all the same absolutely."

—artist Josef Albers (1888–1976)

- **Start by writing your answers to these two questions: Describe an engineer based on the attributes of intelligence, creativity, and communication skills.** Do the same for a fashion designer.

- **Look at the engineering design process on page 9.** List the steps an engineer goes through to solve a problem.

- **Reread the section on design in this chapter.** List the steps a designer goes through to design a piece of clothing.

- **Compare the engineering design process to the fashion design process.** How are they the same? How are they different?

To investigate more, look at your answer to the first question. Do you have stereotypes about the people who work in these two professions? If so, where did those stereotypes come from? What are the most important skills each professional brings to their job? Do you see an overlap?

Chapter 4 ▶

The Latest, Must-Have Accessories

ACCESSORIES: WHEN YOU DIG DEEPER, THEY ARE MORE THAN JUST FAST FASHION!

Can your accessory choices reflect both your style and your values?

BACKPACKS MIGHT SEEM LIKE A NEW INVENTION.

BUT HUMANS HAVE BEEN USING FABRIC TO CARRY ESSENTIALS FOR THOUSANDS OF YEARS.

ACCESSORIES WERE USED FOR MORE THAN JUST FASHION.

THEY PLAYED A HUGE ROLE IN THE DEVELOPMENT OF CIVILIZATIONS.

SOME CAN EVEN BE LIFE SAVING!

WW1 MEDICAL BAG

Accessories can be expensive and aimed at the designer market or they can be trendy and colorful, targeting the teen market. They are often used to express your personality and to further support your style.

Have you ever gotten dressed, looked in the mirror, and wondered what was missing? What essential ingredient might you have missed to tie together the outfit you're wearing? Different shoes? New jacket? What about—a certain belt? Maybe a watch or bracelet would complement your clothing and add just the sense of finish you're looking for. Sometimes, accessories are what make or break an outfit.

Fashion accessories are items that are not attached to the garment you are wearing but are chosen to complement it. Jewelry, belts, scarves, and purses are all considered accessories.

Some popular accessories from the past include mood rings that showed you—and everyone else— what you were feeling, friendship necklaces shared with your best friend, neckties worn as necklaces, and scarves worn as headbands. There were also finger watches, leg warmers, and white belts.

As with all fashion, the "in" accessories often change from year to year, if not season to season. What fashionable accessories are trending for teenagers today? It is anyone's guess if they will be around in a year or two.

Some fashion accessories go beyond trending and become, for many people, an important part of everyday life. Interestingly, these popular fashion accessories reveal a lot about what is "in," not just fashion-wise, but in society as a whole. Let's look at two of the most widely used fashion accessories of today—backpacks and water bottles.

BACKPACKS ARE EVERYWHERE

Obviously, people have carried things around on their backs for ages, but the first modern backpack was patented by Henry Merriam (1837–1912) in 1878. And it wasn't called a backpack but a knapsack.

Merriam's knapsack had a sheet-metal frame and was invented for use by the U.S. Army. The metal frame helped the wearer by "lessening the weight to be carried, and at the same time disposing it more uniformly, and leaving the body of the soldier freer and less hampered by straps and other fastenings." Unfortunately, it didn't take long for Merriam's knapsack to fall out of use due to how uncomfortable it was to wear!

Like many engineering and technological advances, the idea was good, but the reality didn't match up.

Take a look at the hottest accessories hitting the fashion runways.

Do any of them fit your style? Why or why not? Do you think these looks were created with any kind of functionality in mind or are they only meant to appeal aesthetically?

paper 2020 trends

Do you consider phone cases to be an accessory?

Luckily, backpack frames have improved in comfort!

Many iterations of backpacks followed in the years to come, including those with light tubular frames that fit the shape of the back (1908), wooden frames with detachable canvas bags (1920), zippers instead of buckles and straps (1938), softer and more lightweight packs made from parachute material (1952), and backpacks made with internal frames (1967).

In 1970, a company called JanSport released a lightweight, nylon daypack for skiing and hiking. The company placed its backpacks in the University of Washington sporting goods store, hoping to target the hikers on campus.

Instead, students discovered them as a welcome alternative to carrying armloads of heavy books from class to class. The trend caught on and soon students everywhere started using backpacks, not for hiking but for school life. Sporting goods companies, quick to respond to the trend, began to design backpacks specifically for the needs of this new demographic.

It wasn't until 1910 that the word "backpack" found its way into the English language. It took a while longer before the word was used to describe the action of using a backpack on a hike or climb, as in backpacking.

Not only has backpack construction changed throughout the years, so have the materials that are used to make them.

Currently, a growing trend is for backpacks to be made from environmentally friendly material. For instance, Fjallraven's Kanken backpack material uses SpinDye technology to cut down on the amount of chemicals, water, and energy used in the dyeing process. Patagonia's Black Hole backpacks are made from 100-percent recycled polyester. Finally, Rewilder, a small company in Los Angeles, California, makes its unique backpacks out of 100-percent salvaged industrial trash.

In addition to using sustainable materials, backpacks today are designed with our dependence on digital technology in mind. Some backpacks come with attached solar panels and a charging port so that no matter how far you go into the wilderness, you never have to be without your phone or tablet. Some include USB ports and some light up at night. Other backpacks claim anti-theft technology, such as invisible zippers that are difficult for pickpockets to open without being caught.

And, of course, most backpacks for students—and adults—now contain special pockets for computers and cell phones. You can bet that as your digital needs change, so will the design of your backpack.

Water bottles contribute to much of the pollution in natural areas around the world.

WATER BOTTLES

While most of us don't wear our water bottles, enough people carry them around that they could be considered an accessory! Do you carry one to school or sports practice?

Not surprisingly, single-use plastic water bottles are bad for the environment. Americans purchase 50 billion plastic bottles each year and, unfortunately, only 23 percent of those are recycled. Plastic bottles are found floating in the ocean, cluttering deserted beaches, filling up landfills, and messing up city streets.

BIODEGRADING

For a product or substance to be considered biodegradable, bacteria or other living organisms must be able to break down the product so it is recycled into organic matter and new life. Discarded plastic water bottles are eventually broken down by sun, heat, light, and water into small pieces known as microplastics. But they always remain as plastic and stay on Earth forever. In addition, this decomposing, or breaking down, of the plastic can take up to 1,000 years.

Plastic water bottles—and many other plastic items—release microplastics into the land or the water as they slowly break apart. These microplastics are often found in the stomachs of fish and animals that have mistaken them for food. In this way, microplastics end up in our food chain.

In addition, plastic is made from fossil fuels, a nonrenewable resource. The process for making plastic requires huge amounts of energy and emits large amounts of greenhouse gases into our atmosphere, contributing to climate change.

Luckily, many people are quitting the habit of using disposable, single-use plastic water bottles and replacing them with the must-have accessory of today and tomorrow—the reusable water bottle. The longer you use the bottle, the more natural resources you are preserving and the more money you are saving. You also know exactly where the water you are drinking comes from.

In terms of sustainability and functionality, the two best choices for reusable water bottles are glass and stainless steel.

Each has their advantages. Glass is chemically inert, meaning that it doesn't interact with other substances and, therefore, won't absorb the tastes of different beverages. The cranberry juice you drink one day won't flavor the plain water you want the next. Glass doesn't contain any harmful substances and is easy to clean.

Making glass products is far less harmful to the environment than making aluminum or plastic water bottles. The disadvantage to glass is that it doesn't hold the temperature, hot or cold, of the liquid inside. It's not a good insulator.

FABRIC FACT

◇◇◇◇◇◇◇◇◇◇◇◇◇◇◇◇◇◇

An entire 17-ounce plastic bottle was found inside the stomach of a monkfish by a fisherman in South Korea in 2018.

Both glass and stainless steel water bottles are 100-percent recyclable.

Stainless steel is another good choice for a reusable water bottle. It is lightweight, virtually indestructible, and contains no harmful additives that are bad for your health. If you get the double-walled variety, the bottle can hold the temperature—either hot or cold—of a drink for a long time.

SMARTWATCHES: THE FUTURE IS NOW

What exactly is a smartwatch? A smartwatch is a wearable computing device. It uses the same smart technology, and, in fact, works in sync with your smartphone.

The first smartwatch hit the scene in 1972 and, by today's standards, it wasn't all that smart. Basically, it was a digital watch. And you had to push a button to see the time. But in the world of technology, it was a game-changer.

Considering how many people are using reusable water bottles, companies are upping their game by designing not only functional but also beautiful water bottles.

Why is it important to avoid single-use plastic water bottles? Look at these infographics!

How do infographics sometimes make information clearer than long paragraphs of text? What design features do infographics use to help an audience understand them?

Daily Infographic water bottle

Fast forward to today: A smartwatch gives its wearer a lot of connectivity in a small package. Oh, it tells the time, too. You don't even have to push a button! It is a digital tool to help you navigate your daily life.

There are two general types of smartwatches. One is an all-purpose device that serves as a support system for your phone while actually allowing you to keep it in your pocket. It has apps, music, fitness tracking, text-messaging capability, digital game-playing ability, and more.

The other type of smartwatch is one that has a single dedicated function and thus supports only the apps related to that purpose. For instance, the smartwatch for hikers has GPS, tracks your steps, keeps tabs on your heartrate, and shows your elevation.

In 2010, Apple, Sony, and Samsung introduced the first modern smartwatches.

The public reaction, in terms of sales, was underwhelming. Since then, however, things have changed. U.S. smartwatch sales grew from 9 million sold in 2016 to 20.1 million sold in 2019.

But can smartwatches really be considered fashionable? Sure! Smartwatch makers are partnering with designers to make sleeker, more attractive smartwatches. But be warned—they come at a steep price.

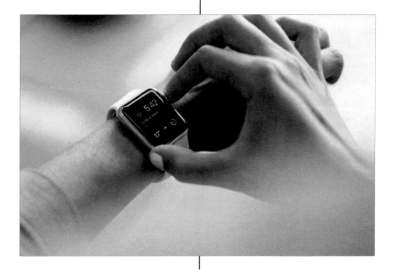

Price is one of the major drawbacks of smartwatches. All of that connectivity and access isn't cheap. Even the less expensive models are sold at a price that many can't afford. Also, in order to have a smartwatch, one must own a smartphone, which comes with its own costs.

A second drawback of smartwatch ownership is the limited battery life. For instance, the battery life for the Apple Watch Series 4 is 18 hours. If you depend on your smartwatch when you are hiking and can't recharge it every day, it might not actually be of use.

In 2020, the COVID-19 pandemic further boosted sales of smartwatches. The reality of working from home has created an increase in the need for remote connectivity and networking capability.

BEAUTIFUL BRACELETS

With all of this talk about functional, useful accessories, let's not forget that, traditionally, the function of most accessories was to provide beauty, sparkle, or bling for the wearer. One type of accessory that has been around almost as long as there have been people to wear them is bracelets.

Archaeologists have found evidence that people wore bracelets in Egypt, Mesopotamia, and China. The early bracelets were made of natural resources such as grasses, thin tree limbs, and shells. As technology progressed, bracelets were made from copper and bronze. By 2680 BCE, Egyptians were decorating bracelets made from gold and silver with semiprecious stones.

In the early days, bracelets were gender neutral. They were worn as decorative accessories by some and for protection by others, such as Greek and Roman soldiers, who wore wide leather and metal cuffs as part of their uniform.

FABRIC FACT

During the twentieth century, bracelets came in all shapes, sizes, and price ranges, with many being massed produced and therefore affordable for everyone.

During the Middle Ages, the bracelet fell out of fashion, but it was brought back in the seventeenth century when women began wearing ribbons and thin bangles as fashion accessories. By the nineteenth century, bracelet chains decorated with charms became popular.

Today, once again, the bracelet has become a gender-neutral accessory. As the green-living movement has grown, so has the demand for accessories made out of natural materials such as wooden beads or braided twine. In addition, bracelets have become more than a fashion accessory. Many people wear bracelets to support social causes or to show group identity. You might wear a pink band to support awareness for breast cancer, while a rainbow-colored bracelet signals gay pride.

Whether you are considering the best eco-friendly backpack to purchase or a water bottle that has the right features to fit your particular needs, remember how these unique accessories came about. Different sports companies worked with and supported the research of scientists and engineers to produce better, healthier products.

We see science and engineering behind the innovations of the SpinDye process and in the creation of machines and manufacturing processes that can turn industrial trash into reusable fiber for the Rewilder backpack. The science and engineering behind technology come into play with the latest features, such as solar panels embedded in backpacks or double-walled stainless steel water bottles.

Now, let's turn our attention to everyone's favorite footwear—sneakers!

KEY QUESTIONS

- Do you wear any accessories? Do they have any special meaning for you?
- How are backpacks and reusable water bottles different from traditional accessories?
- How does the growing use of backpacks and reusable water bottles reflect our society's changing lifestyles and values?
- What are some changes being made to backpacks to make them more eco-friendly?

TEXT TO WORLD

Backpacks started out as tools for hikers and campers. What are some other things that started as specialty items and were eventually used by lots of different people doing different things?

MAKE A DIFFERENCE

Nelson Mandela (1918–2013), the South African freedom fighter and politician, said, "Education is the most powerful weapon you can use to change the world." Maybe you already knew about the dangers of single-use plastic. Maybe you are just learning now. Either way, it is a good time to educate those in your circle of family and friends who don't know. By designing your own infographic, you can share important information visually and quickly, showing how each individual piece of data relates to all the other pieces in an interesting, colorful, easy-to-understand presentation.

- **Take a quick survey of your friends and family.** How many of them consistently use recyclable water bottles? If not, why not? Knowing your audience and their reasons will help you create an infographic to address their specific concerns.

- **Do some research and find important facts about the environmental effects of plastic water bottle usage.** University and government websites are usually the best places to find reliable information. Decide which facts are most compelling. Think about your audience. Who are you going to share this information with?

- **Look up infographics on subjects you already know about to get an idea of what you want yours to look like.** Do you want to use lots of color or keep it more visually simple? How many facts do you want to include? What kind of font do you think would work best for your topic?

- **Get started.** You can create your infographic by hand, using your own symbols and art, or you can do it on one of the free infographic websites available on the internet.

To investigate more, try to be brave! Present your infographic to those who need to be educated about the dangers of using single-use plastic water bottles. Do you get the reaction you were hoping for? What can you do to improve your infographic so people will better understand the problem of single-use plastic?

Inquire & Investigate

Write down what you think each word means. What root words can you find to help you? What does the context of the word tell you?

climate change, **demographic**, **functionality**, **inert**, **iteration**, **microplastics**, and **resource**.

Compare your definitions with those of your friends or classmates. Did you all come up with the same meanings? Turn to the text and glossary if you need help.

IF MY BACKPACK AND WATER BOTTLE COULD TALK

How many hours in your typical day? If you are like most people, your backpack and water bottle spend most of those hours at your side, going everywhere you go. They go with you to class, to the library, to after-school activities, and back home again. What story would they tell about a typical day in your life?

- **Choose a typical day in your life.** It doesn't need to be a special event day, just a regular day when you get up and go to school. Break it down hour by hour, writing a quick note about what you do during each of those hours.

- **Add information about your backpack and water bottle.** Which hours do they go with you? Where are they when you aren't using them? Where do they sit when you are at school? Do you throw them around or treat them gently?

- **Tell the story of your day in hourly panels from the point of view of your eco-friendly accessories!** How do their daily experiences contribute to their design?

To investigate more, get creative and illustrate your story. Take photos of your accessories throughout the day in their various settings and use those photos as models for comic book panels. Did you learn anything new, seeing your daily life from another viewpoint?

Chapter 5 ▶
Simply Sensational Sneakers

How does technology figure into sneaker design and manufacturing?

Your clothing choices offer a story to people you meet. What story does your choice of sneakers tell about you?

Sneakers, tennis shoes, gym shoes, tennies, trainers, kicks—athletic shoes have gone by many different names and through many different versions throughout the years. At first, sneakers were mainly for athletic use. As time went on, sneakers were also made and marketed as fashionable-yet-comfortable everyday wear.

Today, athletic shoes are everywhere. Look around the next time you go to a store or park—old and young alike are striding around in sneakers. Do a quick tally as you walk through the halls of your school. How many of your schoolmates wear athletic shoes every day? You might even see sneakers on the red carpet for fancy Hollywood events or on fashion runways in New York and Paris.

Sneakers are everywhere and on everyone. But why? How did this shoe become such a global phenomenon?

Maybe one reason is that sneakers have a lot of benefits in a perfect package. They offer fashion, status, and cultural links to music and sports celebrities. They also, thanks to advances in science, engineering, and technology, offer better performance in your sport of choice as well as greater comfort in your day-to-day life.

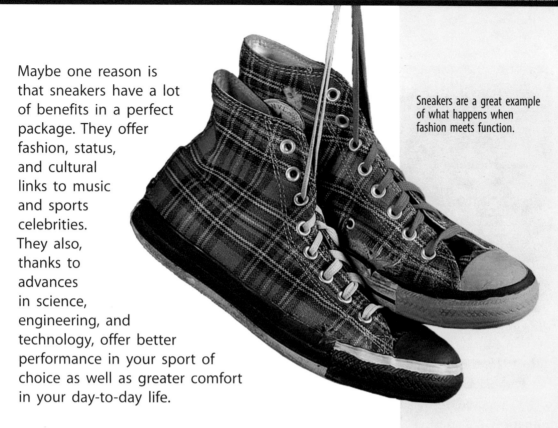

Sneakers are a great example of what happens when fashion meets function.

FIRST STEPS: EARLY SNEAKERS

The first truly modern sneakers did not appear on the scene until the beginning of the 1900s. We can thank an American inventor's refusal to give up on his dream and the societal changes brought about by the Industrial Revolution.

In the early 1820s, natural rubber products such as life preservers, galoshes, and rubber raincoats were widespread in the United States. However, by the end of the 1820s, it was clear that this stretchable, waterproof material was no good for these products. It melted into a pile of goo in hot weather and hardened and cracked during cold weather.

Enter Charles Goodyear (1800–1860), a self-taught chemist and manufacturing engineer. He became obsessed with discovering a way to make this remarkable substance functional.

In 2015, sales of sneakers in the United States topped $36.3 billion!

After many years of experimentation with rubber, during which Goodyear put his family in debt, spent time in debtor's prison, and traveled around the country looking for investors to support his experiments, he finally figured out the solution. In one experiment, he added sulfur to his rubber mixture. When it boiled over onto a hot stove, it did not burn. Instead, the mixture became solid and yet pliable, similar to leather. Goodyear knew he was on the right track.

After several more years of work, he created the chemical process, which he called "vulcanization," to make the natural rubber we know today. In 1844, he received a patent for his work.

In 1916, the United Rubber Company focused on the production of a sneaker for children that it called Keds. The white, canvas, lace-up shoe was the leading brand of children's sneakers for decades. Do you own a pair of Keds today?

Unfortunately for Goodyear, he was not as good in business as he was in science.

He never made money on his invention, although other companies used his discovery to make fortunes.

Shortly after Goodyear died in 1860, rubber companies began making shoes with rubber soles and lightweight or leather uppers. In England, these shoes were called plimsolls. In the United States, they were called sneaks or sneakers and people wore them for sport.

A women's Keds sneaker from 1916

By the early 1900s, interest in this type of shoe took off. With the switch to an industrial economy, people moved from farms to cities and had more money and more time off from work. Plus, by the late 1800s, child labor laws were passed to keep children in school and out of factories. Kids were more involved in sports such as basketball, football, and tennis. And those kids needed appropriate footwear.

In 1917, a competing shoe company released the Converse All-Star high-top canvas sneaker for aspiring basketball players. In a brilliant marketing move, in 1921, the company hired NBA basketball star Chuck Taylor (1901–1969) as a salesman. Taylor traveled the country promoting the shoes and teaching basketball. He also suggested ways to make the shoes even better. Taylor was such a success that in 1924, Converse added his signature to a circular patch on the ankle of the shoe.

For many years, "Chucks" were synonymous with basketball shoes.

Do you have different shoes for basketball and running? In Germany, a young man named Adolf "Adi" Dassler (1900–1978) made shoes in his mother's bathroom. Although he mostly sold everyday shoes, his real passion was for making shoes specifically for running and soccer.

In 1923, Adi's older brother, Rudolph (1898–1974), joined him, and together they formed their own shoe company, Gebruder Dassler. They focused on sports shoes, and by the time the 1936 Olympics were held in Berlin, Germany, most of the German runners were wearing Dassler running shoes. But Adi Dassler wanted more.

The name Keds is said to have been created by combining the words *kid* and *ped*, which is the Latin root word for "foot."

Even though Charles Goodyear didn't reap the financial rewards of his discovery, he wasn't bitter, "I am not disposed to complain that I have planted, and others have gathered the fruits." To understand the importance of Goodyear's discovery, look at this enactment of his work.

Can you think of other inventors and innovators who had a huge impact on the world but did not live to see it?

Goodyear invention rubber
Jordan

Jesse Owens at the Berlin Olympics, 1936

Showing up at the Olympic Village, he hoped to persuade Jesse Owens (1913–1918), already a well-known, successful track star, to wear his shoes. It worked. On the Olympic podium, Owens accepted at least one of his four gold medals wearing Dassler track shoes.

After World War II, Adi and his brother had a falling out. In 1948, they split up their business. Adi started a new shoe company, naming it Adidas, while Rudolf started a shoe company he named Puma. One of Adi's important innovations was the development of screw-in, interchangeable spikes for the soles of sneakers, an invention that led to Adidas's decades-long domination of the soccer cleat market. Have you ever had a pair of Adidas cleats?

MORE SNEAKER SUCCESS!

One of the most famous sneaker stories, encompassing both brilliant marketing and serious science, is the story of Nike.

It all started in the early 1960s, when Phil Knight (1938–) attended business school in California and had an assignment to create a fictional business. Thinking back to the time he ran track for the University of Oregon, Knight remembered his coach, Bill Bowerman (1911–1999), modifying old shoes with refitted parts to improve runners' performance.

As a Black athlete, Jesse Owens faced incredible prejudice at the 1936 Olympics in pre-World War II Germany. Despite the pressure, he became the first American to win four gold medals in track and field in a single Olympics. Read more about the importance of Owens's success.

What impact did his success have on American society?

Biography Owens Hitler

Knight knew that Bowerman's recommendation of specific shoes to other coaches improved sales for that brand. Knight's business idea was to create a U.S.-based shoe company that would distribute low-cost, high-tech running shoes made in Japan. He hypothesized that his ties to Bowerman would give him a leg up when selling to the high school and college track community.

Knight graduated from Stanford and tried some other jobs, but soon came back to his graduate school business idea. He visited the headquarters for the Onitsuka shoe company in Japan and left with a contract to distribute its Tiger running shoes in the United States. Bowerman joined Knight as a business partner and, on January 25, 1964, the Blue Ribbon Sports company was off and running.

As time passed, Bowerman continued to work on improving shoe design for his runners and passed on his ideas for improvements to Onitsuka. Eventually, though, Knight and Bowerman wanted to make and sell their own shoes.

RUBBER TREES

Most rubber products today are made from synthetic rubber. The type of rubber Goodyear developed was natural rubber. Natural rubber is made from the milky, white liquid that oozes from some plants when you cut into them. This liquid is called latex, and as many as 200 plants worldwide produce it.

Have you ever ripped open a dandelion stem? That's latex! However, more than 99 percent of the world's natural rubber is produced from a tree species called *Hevea brasiliensis*. This is a major problem, because the survival of the rubber tree is severely threatened by climate change, disease, and overuse.

On May 31, 1971, the pair officially cut ties with Onitsuka (which later became Asics) and Blue Ribbon Sports became Nike, named after the Greek winged goddess of victory.

Their timing was perfect. The jogging craze hit in the early 1970s. Suddenly, not just serious runners were training on the track, but moms and dads and kids were also hitting trails and sidewalks. Nike developed Nike Waffle Trainers, Bowerman's innovative shoe technology that provided runners a better grip on a variety of surfaces, including artificial turf. The success of Waffle Trainers proved Nike had arrived as a major brand.

The design of the Waffle Trainer was inspired by Bowerman's wife's waffle iron, which was ruined in the making of the prototype!

HOW SNEAKERS ARE MADE

Sneaker manufacturing is a complicated and time-consuming process. Because sneakers are three dimensional instead of flat like a piece of clothing, and because they are made up of many pieces, large and small, the assembly of sneakers, for the most part, is done by hand.

A sneaker has three main parts. The upper is the top of the shoe. The midsole lies between the upper and the lower sole and provides the shoe's cushioning. The lower sole is the part that touches the ground.

FABRIC FACT

Unlike competitive athletics, jogging was something many people could do. By the late 1970s, up to 48 percent of adults in the United States were estimated to have tried jogging. Of those, some had apparently become serious about the sport—the number of runners registered for the New York Marathon went from 156 runners in 1970 to 5,000 in 1977.

The manufacturing steps for each shoe are basically the same. First, the materials necessary for construction are produced separately and shipped to the shoe factory. These materials might include rolls of prepared leather or synthetic mesh for the uppers, gel for cushioning, and synthetic rubber for the lower sole. The material for the shoe uppers is laid out flat for a metal die-cut machine—which operates like a huge cookie cutter—to cut out the different parts of the sneaker.

logo

upper sole

eyelet

tongue

lower sole

midsole

These pieces are bundled together and taken to the part of the shoe factory that houses the stitching line, where 50 to 100 skilled workers are each assigned one specific stitching task. The upper part of the shoe includes the outer shell, the inside lining, the eyelets, the logo, and more. By the end of the sewing line, the upper is no longer flat, but three dimensional.

The final step in the stitching line is to sew the foot-**shaped material, called the Strobel sock, to the bottom of the upper.**

On the final assembly line, the floppy upper shoe is fit onto a foot form called a last that is specifically made for the style and size of the shoe. Workers use steam heat and pressure, along with special machines, to get it to fit. The upper is then glued to the midsole and lower sole, which are made elsewhere in the factory.

To see how shoes are made, watch these videos.

What do you notice about the two different systems? What is similar about the processes? What is different?

How Made 750 Athletic

process Adidas ultra boost

Finally, the last is removed, the shoe is laced up, cleaned up, and checked for quality. Then, it is boxed up and shipped off to warehouses and stores around the world.

Although many steps are needed, the workers are skilled and the work is done in assembly-line fashion so that putting together a single shoe does not take very long. Some factories have more than one stitching line and final assembly line going at once.

FABRIC FACT

How long does it take to assemble a pair of sneakers? On average, a stitching line can stitch about 800 pieces in one day, while an assembly line can assemble about 1,200 to 1,500 pairs in a day. If a factory has two stitching lines going, the factory can turn out 1,600 shoes per day.

BUILT ON INNOVATION

The skyrocketing success of sneakers is due to the constantly evolving technology that keeps offering its consumers newer and better products. But how does this innovation happen?

Creating innovative technologies requires an interdisciplinary approach from designers, scientists, and engineers.

They work cooperatively, each bringing their own knowledge and training. Designers consider form and style as well as function. A materials engineer thinks about what type of material is most suitable. A biomedical engineer understands the physical forces the shoe, and the wearer, will encounter and how those forces might affect not only the foot but the whole body. A mechanical engineer works at keeping the shoe lightweight and sturdy.

While innovations seem like they appear pretty fast, each new innovation builds on science and learning from past mistakes and success. Prototypes are made and tested and improved on until the sneaker company thinks they are truly the best they can be. New sneaker technology keeps consumers coming back and changes how we play sports and enjoy recreation. And the bottom line is that new and innovative sneaker technology is good for business.

Many of the individual parts of today's sneakers reveal technological advances that have been developed and perfected throughout the years.

In 1971, Adidas released the Adidas Americana, a sneaker that had an upper made of synthetic mesh instead of leather. This new material was lighter in weight and more breathable than traditional uppers. The American became the unofficial shoe of the American Basketball Association (ABA).

The addition of air cushioning to sneakers was a major innovation introduced by Nike. Marion Franklin Rudy (1925–2009), a former aerospace engineer, thought that placing something like tiny airbags in the sole of a running shoe would protect the runner against impact.

SIMPLE YET BEAUTIFUL

The classic ballet shoe has been used by ballerinas for hundreds of years. In fact, the art form of ballet began in France in 1682. At that time, ballet shoes had heels. While the sneaker technology is constantly evolving, the ballet shoe hasn't changed since the heel was ditched in the mid-1700s. What was left was a thin, light shoe with a flat sole that allows for maximum flexibility. The shoe stays securely attached to the foot with elastic straps as the ballerina dances and leaps and pirouettes across the stage. Made from satin or leather, ballet shoes are tan, pink, black, or white. Ballet shoes are an example of shoes that are designed and made for a single purpose.

Nike's revolutionary air-cushioning technology in the shoe's midsole first appeared in its Nike Air Tailwind running shoe, released in 1979. The same air system was used in the Nike Air Max 1, released in 1987. The air-cushioning technology is still used today.

The 1984 summer Olympics were held in Los Angeles, California. For this event, Adidas released Micropacer, the first sneaker to put computer technology into a shoe.

A microsensor placed above the big toe inside the left shoe was triggered every time the shoe pushed off the ground.

Nike Air Max

credit: Steve Ling (CC BY 2.0)

The Air Max 1 provided a window into the air cushioning chamber—a pretty cool peek at engineering.

Through this new technology, runners tracked their distance, average speed, and calorie use as it was displayed on a tiny screen attached to the top of the shoe. Back then, no one had fitness trackers on their wristbands or phones!

In 1987, Asics Freaks introduced gel cushioning. Silicone-based gel was embedded into the midsole of running shoes at the place biomechanically determined to receive the most impact. Asics explained the benefits of Asics' gel in a print advertisement from that time, explaining that the gel "has the extraordinary ability to disperse vertical impact into a horizontal plane to absorb shock and dissipate vibrations."

Ideally, this means reducing the risk of injury or fatigue in the body.

In 1989, the Reebok Pump was the first shoe equipped with an internal inflation system. This technology allowed wearers to create a custom fit by using a tiny pump within the shoe to inflate the air bladder.

After two years of research and development, in 2011, Adidas introduced adiZero Crazy Light, the first fully synthetic shoe. At only 9.8 ounces, these shoes were a full 15-percent lighter than its closest competitor.

Introduced for the 2012 Olympic Games in London, the Nike Flyknit was the first running shoe to have a knitted upper. Since it was made of lightweight strands of polyester yarn woven into a one-piece upper, little waste was produced during manufacturing. This appealed in a world that was becoming more and more aware of the environmental cost of producing sneakers and other pieces of clothing and footwear.

That theme was evident in 2016, when Adidas released its UltraBoost Parley shoe made from recycled plastic. Using plastic collected from the ocean, engineers turned waste into yarn and used it to make the uppers of this running shoe, while making the outsole, the bottom of the shoe, from recycled rubber.

BOOT IT!

How do your feet stay warm and dry in the snow? Snow boots! Your boots are made of a mix of materials. Warmth is a job for insulation, usually a synthetic insulation made with microfibers that trap air molecules inside. Snow boots also need to be waterproof. This is achieved by making the uppers out of nylon or leather and the soles out of a rubber product.

Plastic in the ocean is a threat to the environment and living creatures that make their home there. It's also a threat to organisms, including humans, that eat seafood.

In February 2019, Nike released the Nike Adapt BB, a basketball performance shoe that can provide a custom fit for each wearer. Inside the shoe, a custom motor controlled by a cell phone app activates the shoe's self-lacing ability to loosen or tighten the shoe as needed. That's a long way from Goodyear's rubber!

Even as you are reading this chapter, new sneaker technologies are being researched, developed, and released! You can bet that the technology we see in the future will include more smart technology, sustainable materials, and eco-friendly manufacturing.

SUSTAINABLE SNEAKERS

Just like people, products have a life cycle. A sneaker's life cycle starts with the production of the individual materials used to make the sneaker and ends when you either throw away the shoe or recycle it. From the beginning to the end of a sneaker's life cycle, except during the time of its actual use, pollution is part of that life cycle.

Scientists often study the life cycle of products to find out ways and places that a product's impact on the environment can be lessened. The Massachusetts Institute of Technology did an often-cited study of the environmental impact of the shoe industry in 2013. The study found that the majority of sneaker manufacturing's negative carbon footprint comes from the manufacturing stage of the life cycle.

The average running shoe is made up of 65 individual parts that require more than 360 steps for production.

These steps include cutting, sewing, making and injecting gel, molding, heating, and more. Each of these many steps involves machinery, and this machinery requires large amounts of energy. Unfortunately, most shoe manufacturing currently takes place outside the United States in countries that use coal as their primary source of energy, thus releasing large amounts of greenhouse gases into the atmosphere.

In addition, the transportation of the materials from all over the world to a shoe factory takes large amounts of energy. The leather might be coming from Venezuela, while the gel might be manufactured in South Korea. After the shoes are made and packaged, the shoes must be transported to stores and warehouses all around the world, adding more carbon emissions to the tally.

Fashion brands need to take real steps to reduce their carbon footprints by transitioning away from fossil fuels and investing in green alternatives. Consumers need to play their part by supporting those companies that are going green with their own green . . . dollars.

KEY QUESTIONS

- **How did Charles Goodyear's invention contribute to the growth of the sneaker industry?**

- **What role do engineering and design play in the evolution of sports? How are faster paces and world records connected to new sneaker designs?**

- **Why should we recognize the impact of sneaker manufacturing on the environment?**

- **Think of a few innovations in sneaker technology. What role did an engineer play in that innovation?**

Besides putting greenhouse gases into the atmosphere when they are made, sneakers also impact the environment at the end of their life cycle, when you no longer use them. Since they mostly consist of synthetic parts made from petroleum products, they are not biodegradable. Landfills around the world are filling at an alarming rate with materials that do not break down.

However, there is good news in this somewhat bleak picture. Established brands are putting more money into research and development and are coming out with eco-friendly materials and more environmentally friendly manufacturing practices.

As consumers, we need to be part of the solution. Donating used sneakers is one way to keep them out of the landfill, at least temporarily. Buying with the environment in mind by looking for products that are made from recycled materials is another way to cut down on the pollution caused by sneaker manufacturing. Making wise purchases and not buying more than you need is another way to help the environment.

ASSEMBLY LINE KNOW HOW

Shoe manufacturing depends on assembly line production. An assembly line is made up of workers and machines that perform as a system, each one assigned a specific task that they complete before handing off the product to the next person in line to complete the next task. Assembly lines are faster and more efficient than having one person do all the work alone. The Industrial Revolution was made possible because of assembly lines, and they are still seen today in the manufacturing of sneakers. Now, it's your turn to think through the assembly of a familiar product and then work as an efficiency expert to try to make the assembly as effective as possible.

- **Time yourself making a peanut-butter-and-jelly sandwich.** How long did it take? Record the time in your science notebook.

- **Divide the process into individual steps.** Write each step down on an index card. How many cards do you end up with?

- **Gather the same number of family members or friends as steps required to make your PB&J sandwich.** Assign each person one of the assembly-line jobs.

- **Start the assembly-line production at the same time as you start the stopwatch.** How long does it take your assembly line to make an individual sandwich? Compare your individual speed with the assembly-line speed. Which was faster? Do it a few times to get more accurate measurements.

To investigate more, try to come up with corrections to the assembly-line process that makes it even faster. One way to do this is by filming the process to see if you can spot areas for improvement. Do your changes work?

Are you interested in finding out which brands produce eco-friendly sneakers?

Check out this article for more details.

sustainable sneaker brands

To investigate more, do some research and find out how much land the average landfill takes up. Can you find out where the landfill closest to you is located? Remember, landfills do not have an unlimited amount of space. What happens when a landfill gets filled up?

TOO MUCH OF A GOOD THING?

A sneaker can't decompose because it is made of synthetic parts. However, it can break down into elemental parts. But it takes 30 to 40 years for that to happen! This is especially bothersome when you realize that more than 23 billion sneakers are made every year and more than 30 million pairs are thrown out every year. The following exercise will help you understand the magnitude of the problem presented by the world's sneaker obsession.

- **Take one pair of sneakers from your closet.** Putting them tightly together, measure the length and width of the space they take up. Multiply these numbers to find the area.

- **Using that number, multiply it by how many sneakers you currently own.** That is the amount of space that your current shoes will take up in your local landfills for the next 30 to 40 years.

- **Count the total number of sneakers in your household.** How much landfill space will your family be taking up? Your classroom? Your school?

- **In your science journal, answer the following questions.**

  - How many of your sneakers do you wear on a regular basis?

  - What are the reasons that you have for buying/wearing each pair? (In other words, for fashion, for basketball, etc.)

  - Did you need the sneakers or did you buy them on a whim?

  - Could you consolidate your sneaker usage?

Chapter 6 ▶

Fashion: The Good, the Bad, and the Ugly

YOU MEAN MY CLOSET HAS CONSEQUENCES?!

What is fast fashion and why is it bad for the environment?

FAST FASHION IS A HUGE ENVIRONMENTAL ISSUE.

THINK ABOUT ALL OF THE ENERGY USED TO MAKE YOUR CLOTHING.

THERE ARE WAYS YOU CAN HELP!
1) FIX AND REPURPOSE OLD CLOTHING.

2) DONATE CLOTHES TO BE WORN AGAIN.

3) BUY TIMELESS CLOTHING THAT DOESN'T GO OUT OF STYLE QUICKLY.

4) BUY BRANDS THAT WILL LAST LONGER OR BUY SECONDHAND!

Fast fashion is when trendy clothes are made quickly and cheaply, so cheaply that they don't last very long. Does this sound sustainable to you? It can be hard to resist the pull of inexpensive, fashionable clothing, but there's actually a huge hidden cost to fast fashion.

How often do you shop, online or in the store, simply because you are bored? When was the last time you bought a piece of clothing on a whim and, because it was so cheap, didn't feel badly about getting rid of it after wearing it only a few times? Or maybe you threw it away after a few wears because it was coming apart at the seams.

Do you have more than one or two pairs of jeans or sneakers? How many T-shirts do you own?

A dangerous trend in the fashion industry has been building since the 1980s, and really picked up steam in the early 2000s. That trend is called fast fashion. Cheap prices for trendy, ever-changing fashions entice us to buy more and more clothing. And because the clothing pieces are so inexpensive, we tend not to feel bad if we wear them only a few times. Thanks to technological advances, the turn-around time from a designer's sketchpad to your closet can be extremely short.

If you love clothes, that is the good news.
If you love the earth, that is the bad news.

The fashion industry is not good for the environment. It hasn't been since the Industrial Revolution, when cotton came into demand and textile mills spewed toxic chemicals into the air and local rivers. The industry wasn't gentle on people, either, as slave labor harvested the cotton and later small children worked in dangerous conditions in factories to make the textiles.

Conditions did get better as time passed. Not great, but better. Slavery was abolished. Laws were passed to regulate child labor. Conditions and pay for workers in factories improved. Still, toxic chemicals were doing incredible damage to air, land, and water.

Cheap clothing has become the fashion industry's answer to increased demand for new clothing.

Eventually though, thanks to science writers such as Rachel Carson (1907–1964) who sounded the alarm about the negative effects of pesticides and other chemicals, the U.S. government began regulating chemical use to better protect the environment. Also, in those days, clothing cost money and closets were small. Most people didn't buy more than a few new outfits every year.

FABRIC FACT

Today, there are still places in the world where people work in factories under terrible conditions.

Then, fast fashion hit, and the devastating effects of fashion on the environment increased dramatically.

THE EPA

The Environmental Protection Agency (EPA), an independent agency of the U.S. government, was established by President Richard Nixon (1913–1994) on December 2, 1970. Housed in Washington, DC, its mission is to protect human and environmental health through the creation of standards and laws, some of which are tied to the textile manufacturing sector. They cover air, water, and resource conservation.

FAST FASHION AND THE ENVIRONMENT

Fast fashion means a huge increase in the production of clothing. That has greatly increased the amount of greenhouse gases released into the atmosphere. This is cause for concern because increasing levels of greenhouse gases in the atmosphere are linked to global warming and climate change.

Remember the enormous energy use during the production of sneakers? Clothing is similar.

Much of the emissions occur when raw materials are produced for both synthetic and natural textiles. In fact, 65 percent of all fabric production is synthetic and most synthetic fiber is made from fossil fuels. Extracting these non-renewable resources takes large amounts of energy. Turning them into fiber also takes large amounts of energy. During both stages, huge amounts of the greenhouse gas carbon dioxide (CO_2) are released into the atmosphere.

The fossil fuel industry involves extracting oil from deep within Earth and using it in the creation of synthetic fibers.

On the flip side, cotton doesn't take as much energy to grow as synthetic textile production uses, but cotton does require large amounts of water and pesticides. Pesticides release nitrous oxide (N_2O), another greenhouse gas, into the air.

Many companies spray cotton plants with pesticides to keep pests from destroying the plants.

Nitrous oxide has 300 times greater warming power than CO_2. Pesticides also pollute water.

Most clothing is manufactured in developing countries where the primary source of energy for running factory machinery is oil or coal, once again resulting in increased carbon emissions in the atmosphere. Plus, after the clothing is made, it is transported to the consumers who are going to buy the clothing. Since most of the clothing Americans wear is not made in the United States, the extra transportation creates even more greenhouse gas emissions.

Most synthetic fibers, such as polyester, are not biodegradable.

They will never decompose back into organic matter. They will eventually disintegrate, taking anywhere from 20 years to more than 200 years. In the meantime, these piles of clothing are filling up landfills all over the world.

Plus, each time a piece of polyester clothing is washed, it releases up to 700,000 microscopic plastic fibers. These microfibers eventually make their way into the oceans and into the world's food chain.

BLUE LAWS

Not only can you go shopping seven days a week now, but also 24 hours a day if you shop online. In the past, people had to take a day off from being able to shop, every week. Up until the 1960s and 1970s, a set of state and local laws called blue laws prohibited commercial activity on Sundays. By the 1960s, most of those laws had been rolled back. In some states, they are still on the books but rarely enforced.

TRAPPED IN THE GREENHOUSE

The greenhouse gases found in our atmosphere include carbon dioxide, nitrous oxide, methane, fluorinated gases, and water vapor. These gases trap heat and are necessary to keep Earth from being too cold. This is called the greenhouse effect. However, when too many greenhouse gases are in the atmosphere, Earth's temperature increases and leads to a change in climate patterns. Climate change causes an increase in severe weather, drought, fires, and other climate-related disasters. We are seeing climate change turn into a climate crisis in our lifetime, as more people are being displaced from their homes due to natural events related to manmade climate change.

The fashion industry also uses and pollutes massive amounts of fresh water. Traditionally, farmed cotton takes huge amounts of water to grow. The process of dyeing and treating textiles also uses and pollutes lots of water. An estimated 20 percent of industrial water pollution comes from the treatment and dyeing of textiles.

Another problem is one of geography. Many clothes are manufactured in developing countries because of lower labor costs. Because these countries also have less strict or less enforced environmental laws, much of the water used to dye fabric is untreated and dumped directly into local water systems, which affects the health of the people, plants, and animals depending on that water for life.

FABRIC FACT

Ten percent of the world's carbon emissions are attributed to the fashion industry. That is more emissions than all international flights and maritime shipping combined!

Believe it or not, your care of a piece of clothing also comes with a carbon footprint.

Every time you wash a piece of clothing, you are using fresh water and energy to run the washing machine and dryer. If you wash only a few pieces of clothing or wash clothing that isn't particularly dirty, you aren't using water and energy efficiently.

What do you do when you outgrow a piece of clothing? Most people give it away or throw it away. However, the world buys more than 80 billion pieces of clothing every year, far more than people can wear. A lot of that clothing ends up in landfills.

An estimated 85 percent of the clothes Americans donate to charity ends up in landfills!

SCIENCE AND ENGINEERING TO THE RESCUE

Luckily, scientists and engineers are working, often with clothing companies, to come up with viable, creative, and fashionable ways to solve the problems of pollution, overuse of resources, and huge amounts of waste generated by the fashion industry.

Sustainability is now a major focus in fashion research and development.

Sustainable fashion is clothing, footwear, and accessories that are manufactured in a manner that minimizes environmental damage. At the same time, the goal is to respect our natural resources without overusing them.

About 8,000 chemicals are used in the process of turning raw materials into textiles.

An estimated 713 gallons of water are required to make a single T-shirt. Think about that. How many gallons of water do you drink in a day? A year? How many years would it take you to consume the amount of water used to make a single T-shirt?

The hunt for alternative fibers is a good place to start. One alternative is Pinatex, a textile that looks like leather but is made from discarded pineapple leaves. Because the pineapple is already being cultivated for food, this product requires fewer resources to grow.

Sustainability in terms of manufacturing and water usage is another area of development. One example is the technological innovations used to reduce water usage in the manufacturing of Levi's Water<Less jeans. These innovations reduced the amount of water used in the finishing of the jeans by 96 percent.

Making clothing that is easier to recycle or making clothing out of recycled materials is another way fashion is cleaning up its act. Adidas's Parley shoe addresses sustainability by using recycled ocean plastic to make the upper sneaker, while Patagonia's polyester clothing is made from recycled plastic. Since it is difficult to recycle a product made from multiple types of fiber, some brands, such as Nike Flyknit sneakers, are making their products using a single type of fiber, making those shoes easier to recycle when their role as shoes comes to an end.

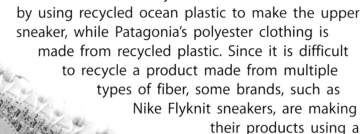

FABRIC FACT

Researchers estimate that the equivalent of one garbage truck full of clothing either ends up burned or dumped into a landfill every second. How many loads were added to landfills in the time that it took you to read this sidebar?

Flyknit sneaker

As you can see, scientists and engineers are working with the fashion industry to create more sustainable, eco-friendly products. Yet, there is still a lot of room for improvement.

For instance, Pinatex, the leather-like textile made from pineapple products, does not use any extra resources in production, so that lessens its carbon footprint. However, because it is coated with a petroleum-based resin, Pinatex is currently not biodegradable and so will ultimately end up in a landfill anyway.

Take another look at a Nike Flyknit. Because of its innovative technology, it requires less energy to make and produces less waste. In addition, since 2016, the knitted upper is made out of recycled plastic bottles, which has helped clean lots of plastic from the ocean and from landfills. But the truth is that removing plastic that is littering our earth doesn't address the essential problem, which is that we have to stop making, selling, and using these plastic bottles in the first place.

Moving away from fast fashion and toward sustainable fashion that's healthier for the environment costs us more money.

The good news is that a study done in 2015 found that millennials don't mind paying more for sustainable and eco-friendly clothing. The study found that respondents ages 15 to 20 would pay more for products that come from companies with a strong commitment to social and environmental causes, up from 55 percent in 2014 to 72 percent in 2015.

You might feel you're doing the right thing when you buy clothing that's made from recycled plastics, but microfibers are still being released during washing and drying. How do we solve the fashion industry's pollution problem? Take a closer look at the problem in this video.

What solutions can you come up with?

Story Stuff microfibers

WHAT YOU CAN DO

As you've seen, scientists and engineers are busy identifying the environmental problems presented by the fashion industry and then working to come up with new technologies, new products, and new understandings of the effects of fashion on the environment. As such, they are an important and necessary part of the future of fashion.

And so are you.

The 5Rs—reduce, reuse, recycle, research, and repurpose—provide a good road map to personal fashion sustainability.

Probably the most obvious thing you can do to fight the negative effects of fast fashion is to reduce your fashion footprint. In other words, buy less! The fewer articles of clothing you buy, the less pollution you have added to the world. In addition, the less stuff you buy, the less you will eventually throw away.

You can also reduce the amount of washing and drying you do. Most clothes don't need to be washed after each wear. By not washing your clothes as often, you not only prolong the life of the garment, but you also use less water and energy. A total win-win.

Cotton production is now responsible for 18 percent of worldwide pesticide use and 25 percent of total insecticide use.

It's not just clothing that can be repurposed!

Reusing clothing is a cost-effective and environmentally sound way to build a wardrobe. If you are like most people, you wear only a fraction of the clothes that you own. You can instantly extend your wardrobe by going through your closet and digging out all those forgotten shirts, pants, and accessories. If they still fit you, wear them!

Remember, washing clothes releases 500,000 tons of microfibers into the ocean each year. That is the equivalent of 50 billion plastic bottles. But you can prevent these microfibers from getting into the ocean.

A report put out by the Institution of Mechanical Engineers highlights that the way you take care of a piece of synthetic clothing can make a difference. They suggest that you wash your clothes at a lower temperature, use mesh laundry bags to catch threads, rely on tumble dryers less often by air drying clothing, or install filters on washing machine waste pipes.

Many people think used clothing is more comfortable anyway!

FABRIC FACT

◇◇◇◇◇◇◇◇◇◇◇◇◇◇◇◇◇

The average American generates 82 pounds of textile waste each year.

Another way to reuse old clothing is to swap with friends or buy "new-to-you" clothes from thrift or consignment shops. A win-win again! You get the thrill of getting something new for less money, saving energy and water, and reducing pollution on our planet.

Recycling clothing is a great way to keep it out of the landfill. Talk with your local clothing donation site to see how they handle recycling. Find a local donation site or charity that takes all your textiles, including sheets and towels and curtains, not just gently used ones.

Only a small percentage of donated clothing is cleaned up and resold to the public.

The majority is sold to businesses that buy it for other purposes. For instance, shredded fabric is used for dog beds and housing insulation. Many clothing companies, including Patagonia and North Face, have started "take back" programs where they will take back your used clothing and offer a store discount in return.

In addition, research your clothing purchases before you put your money down. Why? Because you can vote with your wallet! When you buy a product from a company, you are telling the company that you support its values and the way it does business. So, if you spend your money on clothing from a company that has no plan for sustainability and does not offer any eco-friendly clothing, you are giving the company the green light to continue with business as usual.

Instead, reward the companies that are doing the right thing by buying their products.

You can also use your research skills to check out the label on a piece of clothing to see if it is ethically made or if it consists of eco-friendly materials. Reading the label will give you washing and drying instructions that, if you follow them, should extend the life of your clothing.

Repurposing textiles is a way to extend their lives in a different form. Make comfy quilts out of old T-shirts, use worn-out sheets as drop cloths, and save old towels to wash and dry the family car.

Repurposing can be creative and practical.

Many companies today provide free shipping and returns when you buy online. This practice encourages people to take risks with their ordering, perhaps ordering a size or style they aren't sure of. This results in waste because 30 to 50 percent of returned items never get restocked, but instead are thrown into landfills or incinerated. That equals 30 million units of clothing each year in the United States.

Read how one creative entrepreneur came up with a green alternative to solve this problem.

Treehugger renewal workshop

Aurelie Hulse, a mechanical engineer and lead author of the document titled, "Engineering Out Fashion Waste," put out by the Institution of Mechanical Engineers, wrote that the engineering and scientific community needs to "rethink the way clothes are manufactured, right down to the fibers that are used." She added that it is important to design clothing and create new fabrics with the end in mind—in other words, build the ability to recycle clothing into the design and the creation of textiles right from the start.

How is this different from trying to fix the problems of cheap, disposable clothing after it has been produced?

FABRIC FACT

For every 2 pounds of textiles that decay in a landfill, more than 4 pounds of carbon dioxide is emitted.

As you've read, thanks to fast fashion, the demand for inexpensive clothing has increased. To keep costs low and production high, many clothing companies have turned to developing countries as their source of cheap labor. These countries typically don't have as many laws and regulations in place to protect their workers and, as a result, those workers are exploited. They work long hours, often in dangerous conditions, for extremely low pay. Clothing companies in the West know that this exploitation is going on and yet they put their desire for profit ahead of their desire for humane treatment.

As consumers, it is hard to know which companies are demanding ethical and fair treatment for the workers who make their clothing. Transparency is the answer, because transparency leads to accountability. Once the consumer knows how and where a company makes its clothing and how its workers are treated, they can make an informed decision on doing business with them.

THE FUTURE OF FASHION

Fashion is beautiful. It helps people build a feeling of belonging, reveal their true selves, and add beauty and grace to the world. It is inclusive, bringing people and cultures together. Fashion's existence depends on the knowledge, research, and expertise of engineering and science. And yet, for all its positives, fashion is also destructive. As the second largest polluter in the world, it has a disastrous impact on the environment.

People are stepping up, both in the world of fashion and the world of science and engineering, to identify and solve these problems. As a consumer, you also play a crucial role in solving this problem.

Underneath the beauty and design, fashion is a business. Fashion companies invest time and money and, yes, Earth's resources on products that earn them money. When you stop buying products that are bad for the environment, the fashion industry will stop making them.

Becoming informed about the reality of the fashion industry can help you make environmentally friendly decisions about the clothes you buy. The good decisions you make today will impact the world that you live in tomorrow.

KEY QUESTIONS

- What is the relationship between fashion and the environment? How has this relationship changed in recent years?
- What is sustainable fashion and what problems does it solve?
- Why is thinking of clothing as disposable harmful to the environment?

TEXT TO WORLD

What are you doing to keep fashion from contributing to environmental disaster?

REPURPOSING

Massive amounts of clothing make it into landfills around the world every day. Repurposing, one the 5Rs, is one way to prolong the life of a piece of clothing. The longer that it stays out of a landfill, the smaller carbon footprint it leaves behind.

VOCAB LAB

Write down what you think each word means. What root words can you find to help you? What does the context of the word tell you?

blue laws, **cultivate**, **ethical**, **exploitation**, **fast fashion**, and **viable**.

Compare your definitions with those of your friends or classmates. Did you all come up with the same meanings? Turn to the text and glossary if you need help.

- **Go through your clothing and put aside what you want to give away.** Focus on one or two such items.

- **Sit down with a pencil and paper and open mind.** Brainstorm all the ways that you might repurpose those items. You can also do an internet search to get ideas for repurposing clothing. Remember, brainstorming has no right or wrong answers. You can come up with functional uses or purely artistic ones. Come up with as many as you can.

- **Pick the one that you like the most and figure out how you can put your idea into action and then do it.** Share the results with your friends and family!

> To investigate more, consider that repurposing doesn't have to stop with clothing. Look around and see what other common household items you can repurpose. Keep a scrapbook of ideas for future repurposing projects.

accessory: a thing that can be added to something else in order to make it more useful, versatile, or attractive.

aesthetic: having to do with beauty or the appreciation of beauty.

affiliation: a connection or association with a group.

agrarian: related to the cultivation of land or farming.

analytical: breaking down problems into small parts to find solutions.

anthropologist: a person who studies anthropology, the study of human culture and development.

apprentice: someone who learns to do a job by working for someone who already does the job.

appropriate: suitable or right for a particular situation or purpose.

artisan: a skilled worker who makes things by hand.

assembly line: a way of putting together products in a factory by passing materials from one machine or person to another to complete the next step.

atom: the smallest particle of matter in the universe that makes up everything, like tiny building blocks or grains of sand.

automate: to operate by machine instead of by human labor.

BCE: put after a date, BCE stands for Before Common Era and counts down to zero. CE stands for Common Era and counts up from zero. These nonreligious terms correspond to BC and AD. This book was printed in 2021 CE.

beneficial: producing favorable results, helpful effects.

binding agent: a chemical or other substance that is used to form separate materials into a cohesive whole.

biodegradable: able to break down and be absorbed back into the environment.

biomechanics: the study of the movement of organisms.

biomedical: relating to both biology and medicine.

biomimicry: the study of natural phenomenon in search of design solutions.

bladder: an air-filled sac.

blue laws: state and local laws that prohibit commercial activity such as shopping on Sundays.

capitalize: to make money.

carbon dioxide (CO$_2$): a colorless, odorless gas formed during breathing, burning fossil fuels, and the decay of vegetable matter.

carbon footprint: the total amount of carbon dioxide and other greenhouse gases emitted over the full life cycle of a product or service or by a person or family in a year.

card: to prepare the fibers of cotton or wool for spinning by combing them.

cellulose: a substance that is the main part of the cell walls of plants or the plant fiber in wood pulp.

chemical: the pure form of a substance. It has certain features that can react with other substances. Some chemicals can be combined or broken up to create new chemicals.

chemistry: the science of how atoms and molecules combine to form substances and how those substances interact, combine, and change.

chromatography: a process used to analyze complex mixtures by passing them through a solvent that separates them into their parts.

cleat: a piece on the sole of a shoe that sticks out and allows for better traction.

climate change: a change in long-term weather patterns, which can happen through natural or manmade processes.

cloud-based: computing applications, services, or resources that are available on demand via the internet.

coal: a dark-brown or black rock formed from decayed plants around 300 million years ago. Coal is used as a fuel.

coal tar: a thick, black liquid that is a byproduct of coal processing.

collaborate: to work together with other people on a project.

color theory: the science and art of using color.

colorant: a substance used for coloring a material.

GLOSSARY

colorfast: dyed color that will not fade or wash out.

commercial: relating to the buying and selling of goods or services with the purpose of making money.

complement: to complete or enhance by providing something additional.

computer assisted design (CAD): the use of computers to aid in the creation, modification, or analysis of a design.

conservation: to use something carefully, so it doesn't get used up.

conservative: following traditional values and attitudes.

conservator: a person who repairs and preserves textiles, culturally important items, and works of art.

conserve: to save or protect something, or to use it carefully so it isn't depleted.

constraint: something that holds back.

consumer: a person who buys goods and services.

cotton boll: the seed pod of the cotton plant that fluffy cotton fibers burst from.

cotton gin: a machine that separates the seeds from raw cotton fibers.

cultivate: to prepare and use land for growing food.

culture: the beliefs and way of life of a group of people, which can include religion, language, art, clothing, food, and holidays.

data: facts or pieces of information, often given in the form of numbers, that can be processed by a computer.

data engineering: the part of data science that focuses on the practical applications of data collection and analysis.

data scientist: a person who analyzes and interprets complex digital data.

debris: the scattered pieces of something that has been broken or destroyed.

debt: a sum of money that is owed.

decompose: to rot or break down.

demographic: a group of people who share the same qualities, such as age or gender.

designer: someone who plans the form, look, and workings of a product, including clothing items, based on the experiences of the user or wearer.

die-cut: the cutting of a material into shapes by machine.

digital: involving the use of computer technology.

discrimination: when people are treated differently or more harshly because of things such as race, gender, or age.

drag: a force that acts to slow down an object in air or water.

drought: a prolonged period of abnormally low rainfall, leading to a shortage of water.

dye: a substance used for changing the color of something, such as clothing or hair.

eco-friendly: not harmful to the environment.

economy: a system of producing and consuming goods and services.

ecosystem: an interdependent community of living and nonliving things and their environment.

efficient: wasting as little time, effort, or resources as possible when completing a task.

elements: the weather and other aspects of nature. In chemistry, an element is a substance whose atoms are all the same. Examples of elements include gold, oxygen, and carbon.

emigrate: to leave one's own country to settle in another country.

emission: something sent or given off, such as smoke, gas, heat, or light.

emotion: strong feelings such as love or anger.

engineering: the work an engineer does, using science, math, and creativity to design and build structures.

engineering design process: the series of steps that guides engineering teams as they solve problems.

entrepreneur: a person who takes a risk to start a business.

environment: everything in nature, living and nonliving, including plants, animals, soil, rocks, and water.

environmentally friendly: not harming the environment.

epicenter: the central point of something.

ethical: acting in a way that upholds someone's belief in right and wrong. Doing the right thing.

evolve: to change through time, sometimes into something more complex.

exploitation: benefitting unfairly or unkindly at the expense of someone else.

export: to send goods to another country to sell.

extract: to take out.

fabric: cloth, especially when it is used for making things such as clothes.

fashion: the production and marketing of new styles of clothing and cosmetics.

fashionista: a devoted follower of fashion.

fast fashion: the quick production of inexpensive, trendy fashion.

fatigue: extreme tiredness that results from mental or physical exertion or illness.

feasible: possible to do easily or conveniently.

felting: the process of consolidating knitted material into felt by the application of heat, moisture and mechanical action.

fiber: a long, thin thread that makes up cloth materials, such as cotton or linen.

filament: a single thin thread.

fixative: a substance used to keep things in position or to stick them together.

fixing agent: a chemical compound that sets or fixes something to another, such as a dye to a textile.

flax: a plant with blue flowers whose fibers are used to make linen.

fleece: the fine, soft, curly hair that forms the coat of wool of a sheep or similar animal.

fossil fuel: fuel (such as coal, oil, or natural gas) formed in the earth from plant or animal remains.

functionality: how practical and useful something is, how successfully a product performs.

garment: an item of clothing.

gender neutral: suitable or applicable to both male and female genders, not gender specific.

ginning: the process of separating cotton fibers from seeds and cleaning the fibers.

global warming: an increase in the average temperature of Earth's atmosphere, enough to cause climate change.

global: relating to the entire world.

globalization: the process by which countries and businesses around the world share their cultures, goods, and economies.

glucose: a simple sugar that is an important energy source in living organisms.

graphic design: the art or profession of combining text and images to communicate messages.

gray goods: newly manufactured textiles that have not yet gone through finishing processes such as cleaning and dyeing.

greenhouse effect: the process that occurs when gases in Earth's atmosphere trap the sun's heat.

greenhouse gas: a gas in the atmosphere that traps heat. We need some greenhouse gases, but too many trap too much heat and contribute to climate change.

haute couture: exclusive, high-end fashion.

hemp: a plant with strong fibers that can be used in products such as clothing, baskets, and rope.

hijab: a head covering worn in public by some Muslim women.

inappropriate: behavior that is wrong because it is morally wrong or against acceptable social or professional standards.

Industrial Revolution: a period of time beginning in the late 1700s when people started using machines to make things in large factories.

industry: the large-scale production of goods, especially in factories.

inert: not moving or not able to move.

infographic: a visual representation of data, information, or knowledge.

ink: a colored fluid used for writing, drawing, printing, or duplicating.

innovation: a new creation or a unique solution to a problem.

innovative: new and creative ideas or methods.

insoluble: describes something that cannot be dissolved in water.

inspiration: something that gives people ideas.

insulation: material that covers something to stop heat or electricity from escaping.

interlocking: connecting, attaching, or locking together.

iteration: the repetition of a process.

knitting: the act of forming a textile by connecting a continuous series of loops with yarn or fiber.

landfill: a place where waste and garbage is buried between layers of earth.

lanolin: a fatty substance found on sheep's wool.

last: a foot-shaped form over which a shoe is shaped during manufacture.

latex: a product of rubber trees from which rubber can be made.

loom: a tool used for weaving yarn or thread into fabric.

lower sole: the part of the shoe that touches the ground.

malaria: a tropical disease transmitted by infected mosquitoes.

manmade fiber: fiber that is artificially made by chemical reaction.

manufacturing: making large quantities of products in factories using machines.

mesh: material made of a network of wire or thread.

microplastic: a tiny piece of plastic smaller than a quarter of an inch.

midsole: the layer of material or cushion between the outsole and the insole of a shoe.

molecule: a group of atoms, which are the smallest particles of an element, bound together.

mollusk: an animal with a soft body protected by a shell, such as a clam or snail.

multidisciplinary: combining or involving several academic disciplines or professional specialties in order to work on a topic or problem.

multifaceted: having many different sides or parts.

mutual: common to or shared by two or more parties.

natural: existing in nature and not produced or caused by people.

nonrenewable: not able to be replaced.

nylon: a generic name for a family of strong, synthetic polyamide materials that are fashioned into fibers, filaments, bristles, or sheets and used in textiles or plastics.

organic: something that is or was living.

organism: any living thing.

outsource: to have certain jobs or processes done outside a company, especially in other countries, instead of using inhouse labor.

palette: a range of colors used by a particular designer. Also a thin board or slab on which an artist lays and mixes colors.

pandemic: a worldwide spread of disease.

patent: a legal document that gives an inventor the sole right to their invention so that others may not make, use, or sell the invention.

peer: a person in your group.

perceive: to become aware of something.

pesticide: a chemical used to kill pests such as rodents or insects.

petroleum: a liquid that can be extracted from rocks and turned into fuel or other products.

pigment: a substance that gives color to something.

pliable: bendable, flexible.

plimsolls: an old name for sneakers in Britain.

pollute: to contaminate water, air, or land with harmful or poisonous substances.

polyester: a light cloth made from artificial fibers. It dries quickly after it is washed and is used especially to make clothes.

polymer: a substance with a chainlike structure, meaning lots of atoms are connected.

polymerization: a chemical reaction in which two or more molecules combine to form larger polymer units.

precision machine: a piece of equipment with one or more moving parts whose accuracy and ability to meet very exact specifications are important when creating a finished product.

prejudice: an unfair feeling of dislike for a person or group, usually based on gender, race, or religion.

prêt-à-porter: designer clothing that is sold ready to wear rather than made to measure.

primary colors: the colors red, yellow, and blue that, when mixed, create all the other colors.

primitive: being less developed.

prism: a clear triangular-shaped object that can reflect the full color range of the rainbow.

profit: the money or goods kept after paying the costs of doing business.

prototype: a first or early model of something new.

psychologist: a scientist who studies the behavior and thought processes of the mind.

psychology: the science of the mind and behavior.

pulp: a soft, wet, shapeless mass of material.

raw material: something used to make something else. Natural resources are raw materials.

rayon: a fiber or fabric made from regenerated cellulose.

reciprocal: the practice of exchanging things with others for mutual benefit.

refine: to improve and make more precise by making small changes.

regenerate: to form again, renewing or restoring something.

religious: relating to or believing in a religion.

repurpose: to use in a new way.

resource: something that people can use, such as water, food, and building materials.

retailer: a place or person that sells commodities or goods in small quantities to ultimate consumers.

rural: relating to the countryside rather than a city or town.

saturate: to soak with liquid so that no more can be absorbed.

secondary colors: the colors violet, orange, and green that are made by mixing two primary colors.

sewbot: a sewing robot.

shear: to cut off the wool of a sheep.

shuttle: a tool that holds the yarn or thread that is being woven.

Silk Road: the ancient network of trade routes connecting the Mediterranean Sea and China by land.

slave: a person considered the legal property of another and forced to work without pay and against their will.

slavery: when slaves are used as workers.

smart textile: textiles that have been developed with new technologies that can sense and react to environmental conditions or stimuli.

socioeconomic: the interaction of social and economic factors.

software analysis: includes all activities that help implement production specifications.

solvent: a substance that can dissolve other substances.

spandex: any of various elastic textile fibers made chiefly of polyurethane; clothing made of this material.

spectrum: the band of colors that a ray of light can be separated into.

spin: to twist fibers into yarn or to force liquid through a small hole to make synthetic yarn.

spinneret: an organ through which the silk gossamer, or thread of spiders, silkworms, and certain other insects, is produced. In the production of manmade fibers, it is the cap or plate with a number of small holes through which a fiber-forming solution is forced.

spinning wheel: a wooden wheel with a foot pedal used to make thread out of cotton or wool.

spool: a cylindrical device on which thread, film, tape, or other flexible materials can be wound.

standardize: to make one thing the same as others of that type.

GLOSSARY

statistics: the practice or science of collecting and analyzing numerical data in large quantities.

status: a person's standing or rank in relationship to others, relative rank in a hierarchy or prestige within a group.

STEM: an abbreviation for four closely connected areas of study: science, technology, engineering, and math.

stereotype: an overly simple and often inaccurate picture or opinion of a person, group, or thing.

sulfur: a chemical element.

supply chain: the sequence of steps or processes involved in the production and distribution of a product.

sustainable: a process or resource that can be used without being completely depleted or destroyed or having minimal long-term impact on the environment.

synthetic: something made of artificial materials, using a chemical reaction.

tailor: a person who makes and repairs clothing.

technology: the tools, methods, and systems used to solve a problem or do work.

textile: anything made from fibers or yarns. The fibers can be natural or synthetic.

theme: a central, recurring idea or concept.

three-dimensional (3-D): something that appears solid and can be measured in three directions, length (how long it is), width (how wide it is), and depth (how deep it is, how far back it goes).

toxic: poisonous.

trend: a general direction in which something is developing or changing, a fashion trend.

two-dimensional (2-D): something that appears flat and can be measured in two directions, length and width.

ultraviolet: a kind of light with short wavelengths. It can't be seen with the human eye.

uniform: always the same in character or degree.

value: a strongly held belief about what is valuable, important, or acceptable. Also how much money something is worth. In reference to color, the degree of lightness or darkness of a color.

viable: usable, having a chance at succeeding.

vintage: an object that is old but is kept in good condition because it is interesting or attractive.

vulcanization: the process of making rubber tougher using high temperature and chemicals.

wardrobe: a free-standing closet.

warp: the strong thread that runs vertically on a loom.

wastewater: dirty water that has been used by people in homes, factories, and other businesses.

weaving: a method of textile production in which two distinct sets of yarns or threads are interlaced at right angles to form a fabric or cloth.

weft: the threads that run horizontally in a loom.

yarn: the product created when fibers are twisted or spun together into a continuous strand.

METRIC CONVERSIONS

Use this chart to find the metric equivalents to English measurements. If you need to know a half measurement, divide by two. If you need to know twice the measurement, multiply by two.

ENGLISH	METRIC	
1 inch	2.5	centimeters
1 foot	30.5	centimeters
1 yard	0.9	meter
1 mile	1.6	kilometers
1 pound	0.5	kilogram
1 teaspoon	5	milliliters
1 tablespoon	15	milliliters
1 cup	237	milliliters

BOOKS

Gardner, Jane P. *Fashion Science*. Science 24/7: Mason Crest Publishers, 2015.

Kadolph, Sara J. *Textiles*. Pearson Prentice Hall, 2007.

Keyser, Amber J. *Sneaker Century: A History of Athletic Shoes*. Twenty-First Century Books, 2015.

Mullenbach, Cheryl. *The Industrial Revolution for Kids: The People and Technology That Changed the World, with 21 Activities (For Kids series)*. Chicago Review Press, 2014.

Paisley, Erinne. *Can Your Fashion Change the World?* Orca Books, 2014.

Spilsbury, Richard. *Hi-Tech Clothes: Design and Engineering*. Heinemann, 2013.

Whyman, Kathryn. *Textiles and the Environment*. Stargazer Books, 2005.

Textiles and Fashion: Materials, Design and Technology. Woodhead Publishing Series in Textiles, Vol. 126, 2015.

Yates, Julia. *The Fashion Careers Guidebook: A Guide to Every Career in the Fashion Industry (And How to Get In)*. Barron's, 2011.

WEBSITES

University of Colorado's School of Engineering, this site provides STEM projects for kids, K-12:
teachengineering.org

Statistics on the U.S. apparel market:
statista.com/topics/965/apparel-market-in-the-us

Documentary on environment and fashion industry:
truecostmovie.com/learn-more/environmental-impact

Learn about the wide-ranging effects of the fashion industry on the environment:
greenpeace.org/international/act/detox

RESOURCES

MUSEUMS

School of Fashion Design, Boston, Massachusetts
schooloffashiondesign.org

The Fashion Museum, Bath, England
fashionmuseum.co.uk

For a virtual tour of the Fashion Museum
youtube.com/watch?v=IBX3Yo39Wiw

Fashion Institute of Technology, New York City, New York
fitnyc.edu

SELECTED BIBLIOGRAPHY

Textiles and Fashion: Materials, Design and Technology. Woodhead Publishing Series in Textiles, Vol. 126, 2015.

Eagan, Greta. *Wear No Evil: How to Change the World with Your Wardrobe.* Running Press, 2014.

Hiton, Lisa. *Inventions in Fashion: From Rawhide to Rayon.* Cavendish Square Publishing, 2017.

Kadolph, Sara J. *Textiles.* Pearson Prentice Hall, 2007.

Mollica, Patti. *Color Theory: An Essential Guide to Color—From Basic Principles to Practical Applications.* Walter Foster Publishing, 2013.

QR CODE GLOSSARY

Page 7: psychologytoday.com/us/blog/do-something-different/201304/
what-your-clothes-might-be-saying-about-you

Page 11: thoughtco.com/industrial-revolution-in-pictures-1991940

Page 12: nationalgeographic.org/article/african-american-inventors-19th-century

Page 19: youtu.be/QHgNoSYlhYs

Page 21: youtube.com/watch?v=0KTNYQqSn-0

Page 23: seeker.com/how-the-ancient-silk-road-pioneered-globalization-2272185570.html

Page 24: youtube.com/watch?v=-B4tfduOQ7w

Page 27: youtube.com/watch?v=YYWlevX7Kw0

Page 29: youtube.com/watch?v=MxewR5MzPeo

Page 31: macscientists.com/post/macademics-textile-engineering

Page 32: youtube.com/watch?v=TRlfMhP_CMI

Page 36: ted.com/talks/colm_kelleher_how_we_see_color

Page 39: elizabethancostume.net/dyes/stockholm.html

Page 43: youtu.be/iX83kQ4AkeA

Page 44: prescouter.com/2018/11/sustainable-dyeing-innovations-greener-ways-color-textiles

Page 46: cen.acs.org/business/consumer-products/new-textile-dyeing-methods-make/96/i29

Page 54: artsandculture.google.com/exhibit/1gJCCV3zcuNLJA

Page 55: youtube.com/watch?v=mcwlMsh_g3o

Page 60: youtu.be/5xw_Q_HcNJo

Page 65: papermag.com/spring-2020-trends-fashion-
accessories-2640904851.html?rebelltitem=5#rebelltitem5some

Page 70: dailyinfographic.com/10-reasons-to-use-a-reusable-water-bottle

Page 79: youtube.com/watch?v=y6CJ6ojMT0A

Page 80: biography.com/news/jesse-owens-adolf-hitler-1936-olympics

Page 83: dailymotion.com/video/x7xsiyk

Page 83: youtube.com/watch?v=4J_kxwT9zX4

Page 88: youtube.com/watch?v=NkucZEHUMUo

Page 92: businessinsider.com/sustainable-sneaker-brands

Page 101: youtube.com/watch?v=BqkekY5t7KY

Page 106: treehugger.com/sustainable-fashion/renewal-workshop-tbd.html

INDEX

INDEX